ANGELS
&
DEMONS

ANGELS & DEMONS

COMPANION
Study Guide to *THE THREE HEAVENS*

JOHN HAGEE

WORTHY®
PUBLISHING

© 2015 by John Hagee

Published by Worthy Books, an imprint of Worthy Publishing Group, a division of Worthy Media, Inc., One Franklin Park, 6100 Tower Circle, Suite 210, Franklin, TN 37067.

WORTHY is a registered trademark of Worthy Media, Inc.
HELPING PEOPLE EXPERIENCE THE HEART OF GOD
eBook available at www.worthypublishing.com.

Library of Congress Control Number: 2015946932

Unless otherwise designated, Scripture quotations are taken from the New King James Version of the Bible. Copyright © 1982 by Thomas Nelson, Inc. Used by permission. All rights reserved.

Scripture quotations marked KJV are taken from the King James Version of the Bible. Public domain.

Scripture quotations marked NASB are taken from the NEW AMERICAN STANDARD BIBLE®, Copyright © 1960, 1962, 1963, 1968, 1971, 1972, 1973, 1975, 1977, 1995 by The Lockman Foundation. Used by permission.

Italics added to Scripture quotations are the author's emphasis.

Published in association with Ted Squires Agency, Nashville, Tennessee.

For foreign and subsidiary rights, contact rights@worthypublishing.com.

ISBN: 978-1-61795-610-2

Cover Design: Christopher Tobias, Tobias' Outerwear for Books
Interior Design and Typesetting: Bart Dawson

Printed in the United States of America
15 16 17 18 LBM 8 7 6 5 4 3 2 1

CONTENTS

Will God indeed dwell on the earth?

Behold, heaven [the First and Second Heavens]

and the heaven of heavens [the Third Heaven]

cannot contain You.

—1 Kings 8:27

A Word from Pastor Hagee

Since the publication of *The Three Heavens: Angels, Demons, and What Lies Ahead*, I have received numerous requests for a companion guide from those who are eager to learn more. *Angels and Demons: A Companion Study Guide to The Three Heavens* will continue to explore the Three Heavens, as presented in Scripture. We live in a world filled with supernatural warfare that staggers the mind. It is imperative that believers are familiar with its existence so we can counter its destructive effects through the power found in the Word of God.

The Bible clearly indicates that there are three heavens, each one higher than the other.

The First Heaven, which we will explore, is the heaven we can see with our natural eyes. It includes the sun, the stars, and the sky that presented the phenomenon of the Four Blood Moons. The existence of the First Heaven presents sufficient testimony of the majesty of God. Paul described it thus: "For since the creation of the world His invisible attributes are clearly seen, being understood by the things that are made, even His eternal power and Godhead, so that they are without excuse" (Romans 1:20). Paul is saying that anyone who looks up to the skies and observes God's creation has to acknowledge that there is Someone greater than man who designed the world. If there's a thought, there's a thinker. If there's a plan, there's a planner. If there's a design, there is a designer. God Almighty is the Creator of the heavens and the earth. He is the God who rules the universe and the majesty of the expanse of the First Heaven with all His power and glory!

Next, our journey into the supernatural will take us into the Second Heaven, where Satan rules and reigns. Satan has a Kingdom that is inhabited by his fallen angels and demonic legions that roam the earth (Revelation 2:12–13). Demons are real. Jesus spent 25 percent of His earthly ministry casting out evil spirits. The Bible reveals that demons have personality, purpose, and power. Their objective is to destroy you, your family, your marriage, your health, and your future. Demons can and do control the lives of people who are not covered by the blood of Jesus Christ.

Finally, we will study the biblical evidence of the highest heaven—what Paul refers to as the Third Heaven (2 Corinthians 12:2–4). The Third Heaven is Paradise, where God rules and reigns with His holy angels and the righteous. When Jesus was hanging on the cross He looked to the thief and promised, "Assuredly, I say to you, today you will be with Me in Paradise" (Luke 23:43). Paradise and the Third Heaven are the same place. The Bible says that your last breath on earth is your first breath in the Third Heaven. The very moment you are "absent from the body," you are "present with the Lord" (2 Corinthians 5:8)!

I have written this companion study guide for those of you who desire to go further in the study of the Three Heavens, who want to understand the spiritual forces at work on the earth, and who want to learn practical ways to be free from demonic influence.

It is my prayer that God will open your eyes and heart to a deeper understanding of the things He has revealed in His Word about the Three Heavens.

Heavenly Father, as I begin this deeper study into the Three Heavens, I humbly ask that You continue to reveal the truth of Your Word. May I walk in the confidence of knowing that You and You alone are God and the Creator of the heavens and of the earth. Grant me Your wisdom and understanding, and bless this time as I separate myself from the distractions of this world and bring every thought captive to the obedience of Christ. I ask this in the authority of Your mighty name. Amen.

How to Use This Companion Study Guide

Welcome to the companion study guide to *The Three Heavens: Angels, Demons, and What Lies Ahead,* by Pastor John Hagee. This companion resource is written for those who are interested in the Three Heavens and who want to expand their understanding of what the Bible reveals regarding them.

Everyone reading *Angels and Demons: A Companion Study Guide to The Three Heavens* should first read *The Three Heavens* book. This will greatly enhance your experience of the study questions and bonus material. To reinforce the integration of this companion resource with *The Three Heavens* book, this study guide features direct quotes from *The Three Heavens.* All direct quotes from the book are set in italics, for easy reference.

The design of *Angels and Demons: A Companion Study Guide to The Three Heavens* enables this resource to be used effectively by individuals or by groups. The material is divided into two sections. Part 1 is an eight-week study guide that contains insights, reflections, and discussion questions to guide you through *The Three Heavens* book and to help you apply what you have learned.

Part 2 contains bonus material that provides more detailed teaching about topics that are mentioned in *The Three Heavens.* Readers can either use part 2 in conjunction with the eight-week study, as directed in the study sessions, or read these chapters separately to discover further insights on these intriguing subjects.

How to Use Part 1

The following are some suggested steps to maximize part 1 as an eight-week study guide for individual or group use.

Individual Use

- Begin each study session with prayer, asking God to give you insight and wisdom.
- Make sure you have your Bible, a pen, and a personal journal before you begin the study questions.
- Turn to the opening page of that week's session and reflect on the featured quote from *The Three Heavens*.
- For the fullest experience of this study guide, reread assigned chapters in *The Three Heavens* in their entirety.
- Read and underline in your Bible the "Key Verse" listed for that week's session.
- Read and reflect on the "Key Passage from *The Three Heavens*." Underline any words or phrases in the passage that stand out to you.
- Take your time and read through the "Questions for Personal Study" for each session. Think through the questions, quotes from *The Three Heavens*, and the word and topical studies. Answer each question honestly and prayerfully.
- Write down your responses in the space provided. This study guide is intended to be an interactive tool to help you experience the truths of God's Word. Record additional insights or reflections in your personal journal.
- Look up all the Scripture references given. Read them in context. Allow the Holy Spirit to speak to you through the reading of His Word.
- Read through the "Questions for Group Discussion"

and think through your answers. Jot down any thought-provoking insights in the margins or in your journal.

- Close your week of study with prayer, using the words of the suggested prayer at the end of each session or your own.

- Reflect on what you have learned in each week's session by following through on the suggestions in the "Action Points" section. Remember: study without application is fruitless.

- After you have completed all eight sessions of the study contained in part 1, consider organizing and leading a study group through the questions you have answered and applied.

STUDY GROUPS

- If you are leading a study group, prepare in advance for each week's discussion by setting aside time to read through the session's assigned chapters. Then answer the "Questions for Personal Study" for your own benefit and insight. Finally, after answering and reviewing the "Questions for Group Discussion," you will then have gained personal insight that will enhance your ability to lead a thought-filled discussion of that week's material.

- If you are able, you may want to consider working a couple of lessons ahead to get an idea of the overall direction of the study.

- Confirm that each member has a copy of *The Three Heavens* book, and encourage them to read the book prior to the study. Ask the members of the group to bring their copy of *The Three Heavens* to each study session so they can refer to the content and make notes in their books as they learn new insights.

- When your group meets, be prepared with supplies for them such as pens and Bibles.
- Begin each study session with prayer, asking God to give you wisdom as you lead and to give each member the ability to gain knowledge and understanding as they participate.
- Turn to the opening page of that week's session and read aloud the featured quote from *The Three Heavens*.
- Ask someone in the group to look up the "Key Verse" for the week in his or her Bible and read it aloud to the group.
- Guide the group through the "Questions for Group Discussion" for that week's session.
- If you don't have enough time to discuss a particular question during your group session, remind members that they can continue to do individual study at home and then share their insights with the group the following week.
- Affirm each person who participates in the discussion, especially if the comment is personal, revealing, or comes from a person who is usually quiet.
- Keep the discussion on topic. If someone's answer veers off subject, bring the study back to the topic at hand with gentle reminders such as, "That's an interesting perspective. I'd love to talk about it more with you after the session."
- Give everyone a chance to participate. If someone continually dominates the group discussion, open up the opportunity for others to participate by kindly saying something such as, "I'm grateful for the very valuable contributions you have made to our study so far. Now let's hear from someone else."
- Encourage group members to write down insights they learn during the group discussion in the space provided on

these pages. Remember, this companion study guide is designed to be an interactive tool to help you experience the truths of God's Word.

- Close each group session in prayer. You are welcome to pray spontaneously, or you can use the words of the suggested prayer printed at the end of each week's session.

- Urge the group members to apply what they have learned by choosing from the "Action Points" section. When appropriate, think of ways you can implement the practical applications as a group.

How to Use Part 2

Part 2 contains bonus material that will enhance your understanding of *The Three Heavens*. This section will help you examine biblical teachings regarding the activities within the Three Heavens and how they personally relate to you. These chapters are an opportunity for further exploration, offering more detailed information on how to recognize and deal with demons as well as a biblical understanding of the roles angels play in today's world as our protectors and defenders and as God's exclusive messengers.

We hope that *Angels and Demons: A Companion Study Guide to The Three Heavens* effectively equips and prepares you for the days ahead as we wait for the soon-coming King of kings.

PART ONE

⚬✧⚬

EXAMINING THE RELEVANCE OF
THE THREE HEAVENS

Eight-Week Study Guide for Individual or Group Use

Week 1
What Are the Three Heavens?

⚜

STUDY OF CHAPTER 1 IN *THE THREE HEAVENS*

....

*We are about to embark on a journey that will take us
beyond the First Heaven—what we see with our natural
eyes—into the realm of the Second Heaven where Satan
and his fallen angels dwell, and ultimately into the Third
Heaven where God rules and reigns over the universe,
assisted by His innumerable angelic host.*
—John Hagee, *The Three Heavens*

....

Prepare for Week 1

- Read chapter 1, "Mommy, God Is Alive!" in *The Three Heavens.*
- Optional: Watch "I See Heaven," sermon by Pastor John Hagee, currently online at getv.org.

KEY VERSE

You alone are the LORD; You have made heaven,
the heaven of heavens [more than one], with all their host,
the earth and everything on it, the seas and all that is in them,
and You preserve them all. The host of heaven worships You.

—NEHEMIAH 9:6

KEY PASSAGE FROM *THE THREE HEAVENS*

Most people believe there is only one heaven—the place where God lives with His holy angels. However, the truth is that our God has no limitation on earth or in heaven. He is omnipresent and omnipotent and has universal power and supremacy over all of His creation—which includes all *three heavens!*

—*The Three Heavens*, chapter 1

⚜

• QUESTIONS FOR PERSONAL STUDY •

CHAPTER 1: "MOMMY, GOD IS ALIVE!"

"I was in heaven, Daddy."

Heaven? Did Jack really die and go to heaven? This only happens in the movies . . . not to our boy!

1. Read the story of young Jack's drowning and resuscitation at the beginning of chapter 1 in *The Three Heavens*. What is your response to the father's question: "Did Jack really die and go to heaven?" Give biblical and logical reasons to support your answer.

_____

_____

_____

_____

_____

2. According to Jack, what did he see and experience in heaven? Read Jack's report of heaven and make a list below of the things he described to his parents.

_____

_____

_____

_____

_____

3. Read the following Scripture passages describing heaven. Underline each specific thing and person described to be present there. Then circle all descriptive phrases (starting with "like" or "as").

In My Father's house are many mansions ["big houses"]; if it were not so, I would have told you. I go to prepare a place for you. (John 14:2)

And behold, a throne set in heaven, and One sat on the throne. And He who sat there was like a jasper and a sardius stone in appearance; and there was a rainbow around the throne, in appearance like an emerald. (Revelation 4:2–3)

The twelve gates were twelve pearls: each individual gate was of one pearl. And the street of the city was pure gold ["shiny yellow"], like transparent glass. (Revelation 21:21)

He was transfigured before them. His face shone like the sun ["big light"], and His clothes became as white as the light. (Matthew 17:2)

4. Compare the verses above to the list of Jack's observations that you made in question #2. Then write out any specific connections you noticed between these four Scripture passages and Jack's description of his experience in heaven.

_____

_____

_____

_____

_____

5. In what ways did the list you made in response to question #4 support or differ from your answer to question#1?

_____

_____

_____

_____

6. Based on what you have observed through reading Jack's story and then comparing his description of heaven to Scripture, how would you now answer the doctor's question: "What do you think really took place?" Discuss.

_____

_____

_____

_____

_____

_____

A LIFE-CHANGING MOMENT
I don't know that everyone believes in miracles, but I still do, and I have the word miracle *mentioned by a number of different people in regards to Jackson's experience.* —Jack Cleary[1]

MIRACLE
A *miracle* is defined as "a surprising and welcome event that is not explicable by natural or scientific laws and is therefore considered to be the work of a divine agency."[2] "No phenomenon in nature, however unusual, no event in the course of God's providence, however unexpected, is a miracle unless it can be traced to the agency of man (including prayer under the term agency), and unless it be put forth as a proof of divine mission."[3] (See Matthew 12:38–39; 16:1, 4; Mark 8:11; Luke 11:16; 23:8; John 2:11, 18, 23; Acts 6:8.)

In what ways did you perceive Jack's astounding physical recovery and supernatural experiences to be considered a miracle?

_____

_____

_____

WHAT LIES BEYOND

We are about to embark on a journey that will take us beyond the First Heaven—what we see with our natural eyes—into the realm of the Second Heaven where Satan and his fallen angels dwell, and ultimately into the Third Heaven where God rules and reigns over the universe, assisted by His innumerable angelic host.

1. Read the above quote from *The Three Heavens* book and write out the brief description of each of the Three Heavens:

• First Heaven

_____

_____

_____

• Second Heaven

_____

_____

_____

• Third Heaven

_____

_____

_____

2. Read the following Scripture verses and circle the word "heavens" in each one:

I consider Your heavens, the work of Your fingers, the moon and the stars, which You have ordained. (Psalm 8:3)

"Look! I see the heavens opened and the Son of Man standing at the right hand of God!" (Acts 7:56)

You alone are the LORD; You have made heaven, the heaven of heavens, with all their host, the earth and everything on it, the seas and all that is in them, and You preserve them all. The host of heaven worships You. (Nehemiah 9:6)

3. Why is it significant that these verses use the plural form, *heavens*? What did you learn about the heavens in these verses? Make a list below of your observations. Be specific.

_____

_____

_____

_____

_____

HEAVENS

The usual Hebrew word translated "heavens" is *shamayim,* This is a plural noun meaning "heights" or "elevations" (Genesis 1:1; 2:1). The Hebrew word *marom,* also plural, is sometimes used as equivalent to *shamayim,* meaning "high places" or "heights" (Psalm 68:18; 93:4; 102:19.)[4]

THE HEAVENS

Read the section entitled "The Heavens" of *The Three Heavens* and then answer the questions below.

1. Where is the First Heaven located?

    _____

    _____

    _____

2. Read Genesis 15:5 and Deuteronomy 4:19. According to these verses, what things can we observe in the First Heaven? What is our natural response to seeing these celestial objects? What was one of God's purposes in creating the First Heaven?

    _____

    _____

    _____

    _____

    _____

    _____

3. What beings are present in the Second Heaven? Who has his "throne" and "rules" there?

    _____

    _____

    _____

    _____

4. Revelation 12:4 is a prophetic passage. According to this verse, what percentage of the angels ("stars of heaven") is present in the Second Heaven with Satan ("the dragon")?

_____

_____

_____

_____

5. Who lives in the Third Heaven? Who "rules" from His "throne" there?

_____

_____

_____

_____

6. Read Hebrews 8:1. Who is the "High Priest" mentioned in this verse? (Compare to Ephesians 1:20.) Who is the "Majesty in the heavens"? What this verse reveal to you about the Third Heaven?

_____

_____

_____

_____

For more information about the Bible's teaching on each of the Three Heavens, turn to part 2 of this study guide and read chapter 9: "The Word of God and the Three Heavens."

So Much to Come

Use the word heaven *and it evokes images of a paradise, a place of eternal bliss and perfect happiness . . . but there is so much more!*

1. What images come to your mind when you hear the word "heaven"?

_____

_____

_____

_____

_____

2. How does the idea of heaven make you feel? (Examples include *excited, expectant, hopeful,* or *apprehensive, fearful, worried.*)

   The truth is that our God has no limitation on earth or in heaven. He is omnipresent and omnipotent and has universal power and supremacy over all of His creation—which includes all *three heavens!*

_____

_____

_____

_____

_____

3. In what ways does the understanding of God's supremacy over all three heavens affect your feelings about your personal

concept of heaven? Since God has unlimited power over all His creation, how does that affect your eternal destiny?

_____

_____

_____

_____

_____

4. As you conclude this week's study, read 1 Kings 8:27 aloud:

Will God indeed dwell on the earth? Behold, heaven and the heaven of heavens cannot contain You.

5. Based on your study of *The Three Heavens* so far, what is significant to you about the verse above? How many heavens are referenced in this verse? What does this verse teach us about God?

_____

_____

_____

_____

_____

• QUESTIONS FOR GROUP DISCUSSION •

1. Upon hearing the story of young Jack's drowning and supernatural experiences, Mrs. Hagee responded, *"I believe Jackson saw heaven and spoke to Jesus."* Do you agree or disagree with that statement? Why? What aspects of Jack's story were significant or stood out to you? Did your careful study of Jack's experience in this chapter, compared to the Bible's description of heaven, affect your opinion of heaven in any way?

2. Consider the following statement from Dr. Sam Zuckerman, the pediatric intensive care specialist who attended to young Jack in the ER and later recounted Jack's experience: *"I have often thought of Jackson. Perhaps he was brought back to awaken all of us to God's wonder and grace."* In what specific ways did Jack's experience affect your perspective of God's "wonder and grace"? How were you personally influenced by Jack's story?

3. Discuss the descriptions of each of the Three Heavens that you learned this week. What was your reaction to discovering that the Bible teaches there is more than one heaven? What questions do you still have about any of the Three Heavens? For further reference, discuss any insights you learned by reading chapter 9 of this study guide: "The Word of God and the Three Heavens."

4. Before you began this study, what images came to your mind when you heard the word *heaven*? What images come to your mind now that you have studied the Bible's teaching

on heaven in more detail? Discuss as a group: what do you hope to learn as a result of your study of *The Three Heavens*?

PRAY

Heavenly Father, thank You for the power and the majesty of Your creation. The earth is Your footstool, and You have strategically placed every star in the heavens. We are humbled by Your handiwork. Lord, grant us wisdom and discernment as we read Your precious Word. We ask this in the authority of Your name. Amen.

ACTION POINTS

1. Go to chapter 9 of this study guide and read out loud the Scripture verses describing the Three Heavens.

2. Jack's story underscores that our life here on earth can be suddenly taken away in a single moment. James 4:14 says, "For what is your life? It is even a vapor that appears for a little time and then vanishes away." If the "vapor" of your life were to vanish today, would you be ready to stand before God? What spiritual preparation have you made for your eternal future? Are there any habits, thoughts, or actions in your life that you need to change in order to be ready to stand before God? If so, confess those sins to God and commit to walking in the light of His truth.

3. Consider the following statement: *The Bible teaches that each of us will spend eternity in one of two places: the "highest of heavens" with our Redeemer (Isaiah 57:15), or in hell with*

Satan, the Prince of Darkness (Psalm 9:17). If you were to die today, what would your eternal destination be? How do you know? If you have not yet trusted Jesus Christ for the forgiveness of your sins and assurance of your eternity with Him in the Third Heaven, don't wait! Do it today.

Week 2
Creation: The First Heaven

STUDY OF CHAPTERS 2–3 IN *THE THREE HEAVENS*

....

God has clearly revealed through Scripture, science,
and the events of history that He will use
the First Heaven as His own high-definition billboard
declaring the things to come.
—John Hagee, *The Three Heavens*

....

Prepare for Week 2

- Read chapter 2, "The Heaven We See" in *The Three Heavens*.
- Read chapter 3, "Journey into the Supernatural" in *The Three Heavens*.

KEY VERSE

In the beginning God created the heavens and the earth. . . .
Then God said, "Let there be lights in the firmament of
the heavens to divide the day from the night; and let them
be for signs and seasons, and for days and years; and
let them be for lights in the firmament of the heavens to
give light on the earth"; and it was so. Then God made
two great lights: the greater light to rule the day, and
the lesser light to rule the night. He made the stars also.
God set them in the firmament of the heavens to give
light on the earth, and to rule over the day and over
the night, and to divide the light from the darkness.
And God saw that it was good.

—GENESIS 1:1, 14–18

KEY PASSAGE FROM *THE THREE HEAVENS*

The earth and all that is in it belongs to the Lord and is under His control. David, the shepherd king, stood under the canopy of stars sprinkled like diamonds against the velvet of the night and said, "The heavens declare the glory of God; and the firmament shows His handiwork" (Psalm 19:1). Yes, the sun, the moon, and the stars are celestial evangelists that shout, "There is a God!"

—The Three Heavens, chapter 2

• QUESTIONS FOR PERSONAL STUDY •

CHAPTER 2: THE HEAVEN WE SEE

The Bible begins its profound description of Creation with these words: "In the beginning God created the heavens *and the earth" (Genesis 1:1).*

CREATED

The Hebrew word translated "created" in Genesis 1:1 is *bara*, which means "to make from nothing." God didn't come to an established earth and stir some primordial soup that was already here. Instead, He made the entire universe—including all three heavens—out of *nothing!*[1]

1. Why is it significant that the word "heavens" (Hebrew: *shemayim*) is in the plural form in Genesis 1:1?

_____

_____

_____

_____

2. In 2 Corinthians 12:2, Paul writes that he "was caught up to the third heaven." If there is a Third Heaven, then what does logic dictate? (Go to the beginning of chapter 2 in *The Three Heavens.*)

_____

_____

_____

_____

The First Heaven contains the sun, moon, and stars, yet it is a minuscule glimpse of God's creative majesty (Genesis 1).

3. When you look heavenward and consider all the things that God has made in the First Heaven, what is your response? It is time that we as believers begin to recognize the grandeur of God's creation. Begin by listing the things that we take for granted.

    _____

    _____

    _____

    _____

THE WORK OF GOD'S HANDS

We have all observed the splendor of the First Heaven and probably wondered about its origin.

1. Read Genesis 1:1. Why do you think this verse is so controversial in our society today?

    _____

    _____

    _____

    _____

2. Why is believing Genesis 1:1—the truth that God created the heavens and the earth—essential for every Christian? Dennis Prager, noted syndicated radio host and Bible scholar, made the following profound statement in the recent docudrama film *Four Blood Moons*: "For years I have made the case that the most important verse in the Bible is

Genesis 1:1, 'In the beginning God created the heavens and the earth.' If you don't accept that don't bother reading the rest. It is all predicated on that [one verse]."[2]

_____

_____

_____

_____

3. Read Hebrews 1:10. What did you learn about creation in this verse? Include in your answer the four *W*'s (who, what, when, where).

_____

_____

_____

_____

Man has tried to conquer the heavens for self-seeking purposes since Nimrod and the Tower of Babel.

TOWER OF BABEL

The Tower of Babel was the center for the worship of the sun, moon, and the stars. The tower rose three hundred feet into the air with a rectangular platform of 4,800 square feet at the summit, constituting a sanctuary for false cult worshippers.[3]

The purpose of the Tower of Babel was to cast God and His influence out of the earth. The people wanted to build a great tower that would reach into heaven so they could have the benefits *of* God without actually submitting *to* God.[4]

4. Read Genesis 11:4. What was the goal of building this tower?

_____

_____

5. Read the description of the Tower of Babel under the heading "The Work of God's Hands" in chapter 2 of *The Three Heavens*. What is a *ziggurat?* What was at the top of each ziggurat?

_____

_____

_____

6. Read Genesis 11:5–8. How did God respond to the people's idolatry and worship of the *created*, not the *Creator?*

_____

_____

God Almighty did not make the moon, sun, and stars for people to worship but to confirm His creative majesty, to sustain the earth, and to divide the seasons. The God of Abraham, Isaac, and Jacob even used the sun, moon, and skies to reaffirm His everlasting covenant with David and his descendants.

7. Read Psalm 8:1; Psalm 19:1; and Psalm 89:5, 34–37. What did you learn from these verses about God's purpose in creating the First Heaven?

_____

_____

_____

8. Read Genesis 1:14 and write out below God's purpose for creating the sun, moon, and stars, as stated in this verse.

_____

_____

_____

FROM THE THREE WISE MEN TO KEPLER

The magi from the East examined the prophecy of Numbers 24:17 found in ancient scrolls and searched the First Heaven for a star that would lead them to the King of the Jews.

1. Read Numbers 24:17. What does this verse say about a "star"?

_____

_____

2. Read Micah 5:2. Who is "the One to Be Ruler in Israel" described in this verse? Where does Micah say this Ruler would be born?

_____

_____

3. Read Matthew 2:1–10. In the space below, write what the wise men did in response to seeing the star.

_____

_____

_____

4. The Bible tells us that the wise men studied the sun, moon, and stars—and when they saw the signal God placed in the heavens they took action by asking Herod, "Where is He who has been born King of the Jews? For we have seen His star in the East and have come to worship him." How should we respond to God's signs in the heavens—the appearance of four blood moons and other celestial phenomenon?

_____

_____

_____

5. *Man has continued to search the stars for what they can reveal about what lies beyond our realm.* What do the stars reveal about what lies beyond the First Heaven?

_____

_____

_____

ASTRONOMY VERSUS ASTROLOGY

Astronomy is the science of studying celestial objects such as the sun, moon, stars, and planets. The science of astronomy has enabled us to learn about the universe and even send people to the moon! Astronomy involves scientific observations of the night sky, tracing the patterns and orbits of celestial objects and thus predicting, based on factual data, future cosmic events. The Bible permits us to study the science of astronomy and to look at the stars to watch for signs of His coming (Isaiah 13:9–10; Joel 3:14–15; Matthew 24:29–30; Luke 21:25, 28; Acts 2:19–20).

Astrology, however, is the worship of stars, which is

occult and pagan. People who make choices based on the stars, such as by reading their horoscopes, are seeking guidance for their lives from things created rather than from the Creator. This is a violation of the Law of Almighty God (Romans 1:20–21; Exodus 20:4). Astrology imagines how the stars and planets supposedly influence a person's destiny. The Bible is clear that astrology is a false belief, with no power to predict the future (Daniel 1:20; 2:27–28). God labels this practice an "abomination" and forbids His people from participating in it (Deuteronomy 18:10–14; Isaiah 47:13–14).[5]

The Stars

On a clear night, the earth's sky reveals only about three thousand stars to the naked eye. However, scientists cannot tell us how many stars exist because their number is beyond calculation.

1. Read Genesis 15:5 and compare to Psalm 147:4. Who is able to count the stars? What did you learn about God from this?

_____

_____

_____

2. Who is called the "Bright and Morning Star" in Revelation 22:16? Why is this title significant?

_____

_____

MORNING STAR

....

The "morning star," also called the "daystar," is the star that precedes and accompanies the sun rising. It is the light that indicates the transition from night to day. When Jesus Christ calls Himself the "Bright and Morning Star" in Revelation 22:16, He is implying that He is the Light who will appear as the current age comes to an end and usher in the Day of the Lord (Numbers 24:17; 2 Peter 1:19).[6]

....

THE SUN

The best-known star in the First Heaven is the sun. The sun lies at the heart of our solar system.

Read the Scripture passage below and then answer the following questions.

> *Then God said, "Let there be lights in the firmament of the heavens to divide the day from the night; and let them be for signs and seasons, and for days and years; and let them be for lights in the firmament of the heavens to give light on the earth"; and it was so. Then God made two great lights: the greater light to rule the day, and the lesser light to rule the night. He made the stars also. (Genesis 1:14–16)*

1. For what purposes did God make the sun and moon?

_____

_____

_____

_____

2. What connection can you observe in this passage between the celestial bodies and the later creation of mankind? Do you think God intended these lights in the heavens to affect or relate to mankind in any way? If so, how?

_____

_____

_____

3. Which celestial light is called the "greater light"? What does it do?

_____

_____

_____

THE SUN

How big is the sun? If you compare it to a beach ball that was twenty-four feet in width, then the earth would be less than the size of a golf ball. The sun generates twenty-seven million degrees of heat, and its energy equals the blast of one hundred atomic bombs every second.

Who created this ball of blazing fire in the heaven? God Almighty! One speck of His infinite glory escaped from His fingertips to create a spark that made life on earth possible.[7]

4. Read Psalm 19:4, 6. What did you learn from these verses about the sun?

_____

_____

_____

5. Read Joshua 10:1–13. How does this historical event demonstrate God's absolute control over the sun?

_____

_____

_____

6. Read 2 Kings 20:8–11. What sign did God give King Hezekiah in answer to his prayer and to show His supernatural control over the movement of the sun?

_____

_____

THE SOLAR CLOCK

When God answered Hezekiah's prayer in 2 Kings 20:8–11 by causing the shadow of the sundial to back up ten degrees, He didn't just stop time—He reversed time. That's absolute control!

I believe the exact amount of time Joshua required the sun to stand still to win the battle against the five armies that attacked Israel in Joshua 10, and the amount of time the sun went backward as a sign to Hezekiah in 2 Kings 20, balanced the solar clock. The God we serve created and totally controls the sun![8]

THE MOON

Science has confirmed that the moon is Earth's only natural satellite and is the most luminous object in the First Heaven after the sun. The moon is in synchronous rotation with the earth, and its gravitational influence produces the ocean tides and affects the length of each day.

1. According to Genesis 1:14, 16 and Psalm 104:19, what was God's purpose in creating the moon?

_____

_____

_____

OUR MOON
....

The moon has a notable influence on earth. Its gravitational pull affects earth's ocean tides, and its regular daily and monthly rhythms have guided timekeepers and navigators all over the world for centuries. The moon also helps Earth have a relatively stable climate by regulating Earth's wobble on its axis.[9]
....

2. Why is it significant that the Jewish calendar is based on all three astronomical phenomena—earth's rotation on its axis, moon's revolution around the earth, and earth's orbit around the sun? (See heading "The Moon" in chapter 2 of *The Three Heavens* for more on this subject.)

_____

_____

_____

_____

EXPLORING THE FIRST HEAVEN
Man's unquenchable desire to "go where no man has gone before" has led to enormous scientific advancements and discoveries.

1. Read the list of NASA's space explorations under the heading "Exploring the First Heaven" in chapter 2 of *The Three*

Heavens. List a few of these missions below. Why are these missions significant? What has mankind gained from them?

_____

_____

_____

_____

2. What are a few of the things scientists have learned about the First Heaven using the Hubble Telescope and the Kepler Telescope? (See the section "Exploring the First Heaven" in chapter 2 in *The Three Heavens* or check out "Hubble Discoveries" on hubblesite.org and "Discoveries" on the website kepler.nasa.gov.)

_____

_____

_____

_____

3. Romans 1:20 says, "Since the creation of the world His invisible attributes are clearly seen, being understood by the things that are made." What kinds of things can we learn about God's "invisible attributes" by observing the sun, moon, stars, planets, and all the things created in the First Heaven?

_____

_____

_____

_____

Millions witnessed two complete Blood Moon eclipses in 2014—both of which occurred during major Jewish Feasts (April 15, Passover; October 8, the Feast of Tabernacles)—and a total solar eclipse on March 20, 2015. . . . The third Blood Moon appeared on April 4, 2015, at Passover. The fourth and final Blood Moon coinciding with a Jewish feast in this century [occurred} on September 28, 2015, during the Feast of Tabernacles.

BLOOD MOON

A "blood moon" is a total lunar eclipse in which the moon appears to be red in color. When the earth is perfectly aligned between the sun and the moon, the earth's shadow completely covers the moon, causing a total lunar eclipse. When this happens, the sun's rays pass through the earth's atmosphere and cast on the moon a red shadow, much like a sunset.[10]

4. Read Joel 2:31 and compare it to Acts 2:20. What two astronomical events does God say He will show us in the heavens and earth before the "great and awesome day of the LORD"?

_____

_____

_____

5. As we conclude this chapter, read aloud the following Bible passage:

When I consider Your heavens, the work of Your fingers,
The moon and the stars, which You have ordained,

What is man that You are mindful of him,
And the son of man that You visit him?
For You have made him a little lower than the angels,
And You have crowned him with glory and honor.
You have made him to have dominion over the works of
Your hands;
You have put all things under his feet. (Psalm 8:3–6)

6. In the space provided below describe God's relationship with, and creative purpose for, mankind. (Examples include: "God is mindful of man"; "Man is crowned with glory and honor"; etc.).

_____

_____

_____

_____

7. After you are finished, go back to the Scripture verse in #5 and cross out the word "him" and then replace it with your name (for example: "You are mindful of John.") Then compose a personal prayer of thanksgiving that lists the many ways God has blessed you.

_____

_____

_____

_____

_____

_____

CHAPTER 3: JOURNEYS INTO THE SUPERNATURAL

Is there really a literal heaven and hell? Is there such a thing as an afterlife, and if so, who will be there? What lies beyond man's final breath? Will we see bright lights and hear angels sing, or will we step into an abyss of eternal darkness?

1. How would you answer the questions listed above about the afterlife? Write out your thoughts below.

_____

_____

_____

_____

_____

2. Have you ever been present with someone as he or she stepped from this life into the next? If so, what was that experience like? What thoughts, questions, and emotions did you experience during that time?

_____

_____

_____

_____

When the sun sets each day, we do not mourn its setting because we know it is rising on another horizon. When a ship sails out of our sight on the ocean, we do not grieve over our inability to see it any longer; it is only getting closer to its port of arrival. And so it is in life—our last breath here is our first breath there.

3. What hope do the examples above give you? Be specific.

_____

_____

_____

_____

4. Read Psalm 16:11 and Proverbs 2:20. What do these verses tell us about the way to the Third Heaven, where Jesus resides?

_____

_____

_____

_____

_____

"It Was Not My Time"

So what happened to Uncle Tink?

Simply stated, his spirit left his earthly body, yet was still very much present in this world. It was not Uncle Tink's appointed time to cross over into heaven.

1. Read the story of Joel Lavonne Hagee ("Uncle Tink") in chapter 3 of *The Three Heavens*. What struck you as interesting about this story?

_____

_____

_____

_____

2. Have you ever experienced a time when reading or listening
    to Scripture verses had a significant impact on your circum-
    stances? If so, describe what happened.

    _____

    _____

    _____

    _____

3. Is there anyone in your life who, like Aunt Vivian, prayed
    you through a difficult time no matter what the circum-
    stances? If so, describe below how your loved one's faith and
    persistence affected your own faith and life.

    _____

    _____

    _____

    _____

4. Uncle Tink said, *"I was not afraid to die. What I experienced
    proved that the easiest thing you will ever do is die."* What
    is your response to this statement? In what ways do Uncle
    Tink's words and personal experience affect your own
    perspective on death?

    _____

    _____

    _____

    _____

"I See Heaven"

Martha Swick was escorted by angels to the other side, where her loving husband and beautiful daughter were waiting in glistening white robes for their reunion just inside heaven's pearly gates.

1. Read the story of my grandmother Martha Swick ("I See Heaven") in *The Three Heavens*. What stood out to you about this story?

---

2. In what ways were you encouraged or inspired by Martha's life? How did Martha respond to difficult personal circumstances? Are there any ways in which you would like your own legacy to be similar to Martha's?

---

3. Martha said, *"Stop praying for me! I see heaven, and every time I get close to the other side, your prayers bring me back! I don't want to come back. It's so beautiful there. Charles and Esther Gladys are waving at me from the other side."* What is your response to this statement? What can we learn from

Martha's experience about the process of "crossing over" into the Third Heaven?

_____
_____
_____
_____

ANGELS, HEAVEN, AND A MOTHER'S LOVE

It was very touching to hear this young boy speak so clearly of his experience with the angels in heaven.

1. Read the story of the young boy, "Angels, Heaven, and a Mother's Love," in chapter 3 of *The Three Heavens*. What was especially noteworthy to you about this story?

_____
_____
_____
_____

2. The little boy told his mother, *"The angels told me to come back to you, but I was so happy there. I felt so good. Mommy, why did you call me to come home?"* If you were the boy's mother, how would you respond to this question?

_____
_____
_____
_____

3. The boy described the angels as *"calling me to play."* What images usually come to your mind when you think of angels?

How did this boy's description of the angels affect your own perception of what angels are like?

_____

_____

_____

"Listen to the Angels"

The memory of Jack's death, his vision of heaven, the effect his life had on the lives of others and the image of Christ he projected has been more of an inspiration to me, I suppose, than anything else that has ever come to me through any man.

1. Read the story of Jack Cash, the older brother of Johnny Cash, "Listen to the Angels," chapter 3 in *The Three Heavens*. What aspects of this story stood out to you?

    _____

    _____

    _____

2. Jack told his mother, *"All of a sudden I turned, and now, I'm going toward heaven. Mama, can you hear the angels singing? . . . Mama, listen to the angels. I'm going there, Mama."* There is little doubt that music played a significant role in the Cash family. How do you think Johnny and his parents felt when they heard Jack proclaim he was being welcomed into heaven by the angels' song?

    _____

    _____

    _____

    _____

3. Jack also described a *"river"* and a *"beautiful city."* Read Revelation 22:1 and Revelation 21:2. In what ways was Jack's vision of heaven consistent with the Bible's descriptions of the Third Heaven?

_____

_____

_____

_____

An Irresistible Paradise

Before she crossed the threshold, the spiritual beings turned to her and said that it was not her time, that she must return to her body, to the earth, to her family, in order to finish the work God still had for her.

1. Read the story of Dr. Mary Neal, "An Irresistible Paradise," in *The Three Heavens*. What aspects of Dr. Neal's story were significant to you?

_____

_____

_____

2. Dr. Neal admitted she had a hard time accepting her patient's death. Can you relate to Dr. Neal's sorrow regarding someone who has died, even though the person told you not to be sad because he or she was going to heaven?

_____

_____

_____

_____

3. Dr. Neal also admitted that she didn't fully grasp the patient's claim to have been in the presence of angels. Have you ever been skeptical of a person's near-death experience? Why or why not? Explain the situation below.

_____

_____

_____

_____

4. Dr. Neal describes her encounter with death as feeling more alive than ever before. She writes of being greeted *"with the most overwhelming joy I have ever experienced"* and seeing an *"irresistible paradise."* Read Luke 16:22. In what ways was Dr. Neal's experience similar to the experience of Lazarus in this passage?

_____

_____

_____

_____

5. Dr. Neal wrote, *"God and His angelic messengers are present and active in our world today and this involvement and intervention is both ordinary in its frequency and extraordinary in its occurrence."* Do you agree or disagree with this statement? Explain your answer.

_____

_____

_____

_____

• QUESTIONS FOR GROUP DISCUSSION •

1. Consider this statement: *No matter how much we try to make sense of all that we see and know, certain realities cannot be explained by human logic or science. There are certain experiences that can only be described as "supernatural."* How do human logic and secular science fall short in their attempts to explain the creation of the First Heaven apart from the supernatural? Does a supernatural origin make something less real? Discuss.

2. What insights did you learn about God's absolute control over the First Heaven in your study of biblical passages this week? Give specific examples.

3. Discuss the following statement: *Everyone will leave this world someday and enter into an eternal home. When we depart this life, we will walk into the next one, for every exit from one place is also an entrance into another. The question we must ask ourselves is, "What world am I entering into?"* In what ways did the personal stories in chapter 3 affect your view of life after death? How did this reality make you feel? Ask yourself the question: *"What world am I entering into?"* What is your response? Why?

PRAY

Heavenly Father, we declare our absolute belief that You alone are the Architect of the heavens and the earth. You are the Author of life and the Conqueror of death. You direct and protect the path of the righteous. Your Word declares that You will never leave us or forsake us even during our afflictions. We praise Your holy name for You are good and Your mercy endures forever! Amen.

Action Points

1. Commit to read and study the Scriptures on a regular basis so you are ready to walk in obedience. If you want to join me in receiving a daily Scripture reading plan, I invite you to go to www.jhm.org, and click on the Resources page to sign up for the Daily Scripture Reading and Pastoral Blessing.

2. Considering what you learned this week regarding the First Heaven, are there any current habits you have adopted that aren't conducive to spiritual growth in Christ? Are there any habits you can incorporate into your daily life, such as taking walks and admiring nature, that will help you focus on the Creator? Write in your journal the area(s) you can change and commit them to Jesus.

3. If you have not yet read John Hagee's book *Four Blood Moons: Something Big Is About to Happen*, get a copy and read it as soon as possible. The current Four Blood Moons will give you a deeper understanding of the First Heaven and how God uses the sun, moon, and stars as His heavenly billboard to proclaim His character and foretell prophetic events. You can purchase a copy today at your local bookstore, order online at BarnesandNoble.com or Amazon.com, or go to jhm.org.

Week 3
Spiritual War in the Second Heaven

STUDY OF CHAPTERS 4–5 IN *THE THREE HEAVENS*

The Scriptures speak of heaven and hell, of the angels of God and the fallen angels of Satan, and of the war between these two powerful celestial forces. We live in a world of good and evil, a world of light and darkness, a world of angels and demons. There is no doubt that we are surrounded by supernatural beings infinite in number and great in power. Their ongoing battles over the human soul take place in the Second Heaven.
—John Hagee, *The Three Heavens*

Prepare for Week 3

- Read chapter 4, "The Midst of Heaven," in *The Three Heavens*.
- Read chapter 5, "The Clash of Two Kingdoms" in *The Three Heavens*.

KEY VERSE

Says He who has the sharp two-edged sword: "I know your works, and where you dwell, where Satan's throne is."
—REVELATION 2:12–13

KEY PASSAGE FROM *THE THREE HEAVENS*

Once banished from Paradise (the Third Heaven), the Rebel of all rebels established his throne in the Second Heaven, or "mid-heaven," where he and his fallen angels rule over all the kingdoms of the world.
—*The Three Heavens*, chapter 4

⚭

• QUESTIONS FOR PERSONAL STUDY •

CHAPTER 4: THE MIDST OF HEAVEN

John the Revelator spoke of a region described as "the midst of heaven," or "mid-heaven," which is the Greek word mesouranema.

1. Read Revelation 8:13. What is occurring in "the midst of heaven" (or "mid-heaven") in this verse? Who is present there?

_____

_____

_____

MID-HEAVEN

The Greek word *mesouranema* denotes "mid-heaven," or the midst of the heavens. It is a combination of the words *mesos* (meaning "middle") and *ouranos* (meaning "heaven" or "the heavenlies").[1]

2. Read Daniel 10:12–13. Describe the battle that is taking place in these verses. (Note that in this passage, "prince" refers to an angelic being.)

_____

_____

_____

_____

LUCIFER

God created an inexpressibly beautiful angel named Lucifer. He was a cherub and the overseer of the Garden of God. He was also wise, the most glorious of all the angels, and the worship leader in Paradise.

1. What images come to your mind when you picture Satan, or Lucifer?

_____

_____

_____

2. In contrast, how does the Bible describe Lucifer before his fall? Read Isaiah 14:12. What title is attributed to Lucifer in

this verse? (Note: the Hebrew idiom "son of" means "characterized by.")

_____

_____

_____

3. Before his fall, Lucifer *reflected the magnificent majesty of God's radiance.* Yet after his fall, Satan's Kingdom is called "the power of darkness" (Colossians 1:13) and is characterized by darkness (Ephesians 6:12). What does that contrast tell us about the source of Lucifer's light? Did Satan have his own light? Where does true Light come from? (John 8:12)

_____

_____

_____

_____

4. Read Ezekiel 28:12–14. How is Lucifer described in these verses? Where was he? Who created him? What was prepared for him?

_____

_____

_____

"ANOINTED CHERUB WHO COVERS"

When most people think of a cherub, they think of a pudgy, baby-like creature. But that's not how the Bible describes them! A *cherub* (plural: *cherubim*) is a particular type of angel. They carry God's throne and cover it from above (Ezekiel 1). Cherubim are symbolic of God's holy presence and His majesty. They are the mighty and powerful guardians of God.

According to Ezekiel 28, Lucifer (Satan) was the covering cherub (v. 14). He was the highest-ranking cherub, the anointed cherub whose position was to guard over the throne of God, while the other cherubs were placed under it. Lucifer's position was that of protecting the holiness of God.[2]

When Moses made the mercy seat and placed it into the tabernacle's Holy of Holies, two cherubim were carved on the mercy seat (Exodus 25:18–22; 37:7–9; Numbers 7:89; Hebrews 9:5). The cherubim guarded and covered the mercy seat with their wings. This earthly mercy seat was a representation of the heavenly temple, in which Lucifer's expansive wings "covered" the heavenly mercy seat, where God's glory is manifested.[3]

BIRTH OF A REBEL

God created a cherub who had free will to make decisions; He did not create the monster that Lucifer became. The angel Lucifer willfully chose to attempt to overthrow God and His Kingdom.

1. Read the following passage, describing Lucifer's declaration of defiance. Then in the space below, write out the five "I will" statements that Lucifer made:

You have said in your heart; "I will ascend into heaven, I will exalt my throne above the stars of God; I will also sit on

the mount of the congregation. . . . I will ascend above the
heights of the clouds, I will be like the Most High." (Isaiah
14:13–14)

- "I will . . . _____
- "I will . . . _____
- "I will . . . _____
- "I will . . . _____
- "I will . . . _____

2. What did you learn about Lucifer's desire through these five "I will" statements? Who did he want to rule over? Who did he want to be equal with? Write out any observations about how these stated desires contradict Lucifer's created purpose as the guardian of God's throne and worship leader in heaven.

_____

_____

_____

3. How would you define *pride?* Write out your definition below.

_____

_____

_____

4. Read Proverbs 16:18. According to this verse, what attitude precedes destruction? Why?

_____

_____

_____

5. Read Psalm 10:4 and Proverbs 8:13. In what ways is pride the root of every other sin?

    _____

    _____

    _____

6. According to James 4:6 what is God's attitude toward pride? Why can God not coexist with the sin of pride?

    _____

    _____

    _____

7. Read Isaiah 14:25 and Ezekiel 28:15–16. What was the consequence of Lucifer's rebellion?

    _____

    _____

    _____

SATAN'S NATURE AND INTENT

Since the fall of Lucifer, Satan is known by many names which not only epitomize his evil nature but also define his brutal and vicious mission to destroy God's purposes.

1. Read the Scripture verses below. Beside each one write the name used for Satan and what these titles describe:
    *   Matthew 4:3—
    *   Matthew 12:24—
    *   Mark 3:27—
    *   John 8:44—
    *   John 14:30—

- Ephesians 2:2—
- Hebrews 2:14—
- 1 Peter 5:8—
- 1 John 5:19—
- Revelation 9:11—
- Revelation 12:9—

Think of it . . . Lucifer was lovingly and perfectly created by the Great I AM. Almighty God had a divine assignment for this anointed cherub, but instead, Lucifer chose a path that would lead him to be branded as an agent of death and destruction who is now known as Satan.

SATAN

The Hebrew word *satan* means "an adversary, one who resists." In the Old Testament, the word is preceded by a definite article, as a title or proper noun.

In the New Testament, *satan* is used interchangeably with *diabolos*, "the devil," which means "one who is a traducer, a slanderer."[4]

2. *When God establishes, Satan opposes.* Based on your study of the Bible, what are some of the ways Satan has opposed and attempted to thwart God's plan through the centuries? (See the section on "Satan's Nature and Intent" in chapter 4 of *The Three Heavens* for a few examples.)

3. Give examples of times in biblical history that Satan was successful in turning people's hearts away from God. (See Deuteronomy 9:16; Judges 2:17; 1 Kings 11:9.)

_____

_____

_____

_____

4. Read the following verses and write out below what you learn about God and His plans:
   - Isaiah 14:27—
   - Job 42:2—
   - Psalm 33:10–11—
   - Proverbs 16:4—
   - Proverbs 19:21—
   - Proverbs 21:30—
   - 2 Chronicles 20:6—

5. Based on your study of the verses above, is Satan able to thwart God's ultimate plan? Why or why not?

_____

_____

_____

Once banished from Paradise (the Third Heaven), the Rebel of all rebels established his throne in the Second Heaven, or "midheaven," where he and his fallen angels rule over all the kingdoms of the world.

6. Read 1 John 5:19 and Revelation 2:12–13. What did you learn from these verses about the location of Satan's current Kingdom?

_____

_____

_____

_____

THE KINGDOM OF SATAN

Satan's reign and influence encompass the First and Second Heavens, but he roams freely about the earth.

1. Read Job 1:6–7. What was Satan's answer when God asked him, "From where do you come?" What does that tell you about Satan's influence and activity on earth today?

_____

_____

_____

_____

2. Read 2 Corinthians 11:13–15 and 1 Timothy 4:1. What did these verses tell you about Satan's influence, not only in the world but also in the church? Discuss.

_____

_____

_____

_____

3. According to 1 Peter 5:8–9 and James 4:7, what are we to do when we are attacked by the Devil and his evil powers? What are some practical ways we can resist him? Be specific.

4. Read Revelation 20:1–3. What is Satan's ultimate end? What does this tell you about Who has ultimate authority over all the universe and everything in it? In what ways does this reality encourage you about your own circumstances or about issues you observe in today's world?

5. *The Kingdom of Satan is comprised of four evil divisions.* Read Ephesians 6:12, and then write out a short description of each of these divisions, based on the information in "The Kingdom of Satan" in chapter 4 of *The Three Heavens:*
   - Principalities—
   - Powers—
   - Rulers of the darkness of this age—
   - Spiritual hosts of wickedness—

6. In your opinion, why do you think Satan has organized his legions into ranks? What is his foremost goal? (See Matthew 13:19; 1 Peter 5:8; Revelation 12:9.)

_____

_____

_____

_____

CHAPTER 5: THE CLASH OF TWO KINGDOMS

There is at this moment a war going on in the spiritual realm that affects every person on the face of the earth. It is the clash of two Kingdoms. One Kingdom is under the command of Almighty God, the Prince of Peace (Psalm 103:19; Isaiah 9:6); the other Kingdom is under the command of Satan, the Prince of the Power of Darkness (Matthew 12:26; Colossians 1:13).

1. Read the definition of "the Kingdom of God" at the beginning of chapter 5 of *The Three Heavens*. What stood out to you in that definition? What did you learn from this definition?

_____

_____

_____

_____

2. Scripture has much to say about the Kingdom of God. Read the following Bible verses and write out what you learn about God's Kingdom:
   • Job 38:4–7—
   • Psalm 45:6—

- Psalm 103:19—
- Daniel 2:44—
- Daniel 4:3—
- Daniel 6:26—
- Revelation 2:10—

3. *Paul listed four levels of authority within God's Kingdom in descending order.* Read Colossians 1:16, and then make a list of these four divisions:

- _____
- _____
- _____
- _____

4. Compare the four ranks in God's Kingdom (Colossians 1:16) to the four in Satan's Kingdom (Ephesians 6:12). Which ranks are excluded from Satan's list and why?

_____
_____
_____
_____

WAR IN THE HEAVENLIES

Picture in the theater of your mind two Kingdoms: one belonging to God, and the other to His great adversary, Satan. One stands for good and the other for evil. One stands for light and the other for darkness. One stands for blessings and the other for curses. One stands for life and the other for death. These two opposing Kingdoms cannot coexist; they are at war!

1. When did this war between God's Kingdom and Satan's Kingdom begin? Was it before or after Genesis 1:1?

_____

_____

_____

_____

2. What caused this epic clash of Kingdoms? (See Revelation 12:7–19.)

_____

_____

_____

_____

3. Where do Satan and his followers exercise their influence now? (See John 14:30; Ephesians 2:2; 2 Corinthians 4:3–4.)

_____

_____

_____

_____

4. What will be the final result of Satan's Kingdom? (See Revelation 20:10.)

_____

_____

_____

_____

INVASION OF THE GARDEN

Satan's initial attack on God's authority on earth occurred in the Garden of Eden.

1. Read Matthew 4:8–9. What did Satan offer to do with all the kingdoms of the world? What does this imply about his belief of who possesses these kingdoms?

    _____

    _____

    _____

    _____

2. Since Satan believes all the kingdoms on earth belong to him, what did he think of God's creation of Adam and Eve and the authority he gave them in the Garden of Eden? In what way does that affect your understanding of Satan's temptation of them (Genesis 3)?

    _____

    _____

    _____

    _____

3. *That old serpent, the Devil, made his way to Eve and employed three strategic tactics against her.* Based on your reading of "Invasion of the Garden" in *The Three Heavens*, briefly describe each of Satan's diabolical tactics:
    - Doubt—
    - Supposition—
    - Temptation—

4. Do you see any correlation between Satan's temptation in Genesis 3:5 ("you will be like God") and Satan's own desires that led to his fall from heaven (Isaiah 14:14)? If so, write it out below.

_____

_____

_____

_____

5. Do you think the fall of Adam and Eve came as a surprise to God? Why or why not? Discuss.

_____

_____

_____

_____

God already knew the Adversary's plan; God knew how Adam and Eve would respond. And in the moment Adam and Eve rebelled, the sovereign God set into motion His miraculous plan of redemption.

6. Read Genesis 3:21 and compare it to Hebrews 9:22 and 10:10. How did the first animal sacrifice (the animal killed in order to make clothes for Adam and Eve) foreshadow a future, ultimate sacrifice?

_____

_____

_____

_____

7. Satan's attack had two goals: (1) to separate humanity from God, and (2) to seduce them into forming an allegiance with him so he can become the god of this world. In what ways did Adam and Eve's fall in the Garden further these two goals? How did God's response to Satan's plans prevent Satan's evil objectives?

_____

_____

_____

_____

MURDER IN THE FIRST DEGREE

God's divine plan of redemption was in place, but it was not acceptable to Satan. In response, he devised a plan to annihilate the seed that would birth the Savior of the world.

1. Read the story of Cain and Abel in Genesis 4:1–15. What were the two different kinds of offerings the brothers brought before the Lord?
   • Cain's offering (v. 3)—
   • Abel's offering (v. 4)—

2. Why was Cain's offering unacceptable to the Lord? (See Genesis 3:17.)

_____

_____

_____

3. Why was Abel's offering acceptable to the Lord? (See Hebrews 9:22 and 11:4.)

_____

_____

_____

_____

4. Read Genesis 4:5, 8. How did Cain respond to God's rejection of his sacrifice?

_____

_____

_____

_____

It is significant to realize that the first murder was over religion—one founded on humanism and the other on faith in God. Sadly, religion has continued to be the cause of many wars and much bloodshed.

5. Read 1 John 3:10–12. Notice the description of Cain as "of the wicked one." According to this passage, who was ultimately responsible for the murder of Abel? What insights does that give you into the wars and bloodshed over religious beliefs that have occurred in the past and are still taking place today? Discuss.

_____

_____

_____

_____

6. Although he orchestrated the murder of Abel, Satan was unsuccessful in ending the righteous line of Adam and Eve's descendants. Who appears in Genesis 4:25? What is significant about his parents' use of the phrase "instead of" (or "in the place of")?

_____

_____

_____

INVASION OF THE NEPHILIM

Satan's obsession with total power prompted him, as the self-appointed Commander of the Kingdom of Darkness, to call upon his evil legions to infiltrate mankind with the intent to pollute the Adamic line leading to the Messiah.

1. Read Genesis 6:1–2. Who are the "sons of God" described in this passage? (Go to Jude 6.) What did they do? What was the result?

_____

_____

_____

These fallen angels came to earth and produced a race of Nephilim, or giants. The meaning of the word Nephilim *in the Hebrew is "fallen."*

2. Read Genesis 6:5. What effect did the satanic invasion of the Nephilim have on the world?

_____

_____

3. Read Genesis 6:11–13. What did God do as a result of this great apostasy and the satanic influence on the world?

_____

_____

_____

_____

KNOW THE ENEMY

Underestimating the enemy is suicide; it is akin to becoming an ally with the opposition for your own defeat. This is why every strategic military invasion is preceded by extensive reconnaissance and an intensive study of the enemy.

1. Read Ephesians 6:11. What does Paul encourage us to do in this verse? Why?

_____

_____

_____

_____

2. According to Ephesians 6:12, who is our real enemy?

_____

_____

_____

_____

3. _Under Satan's command, demons work together to inflict every conceivable form of harm, deception, and torment on humanity._ Why should we be aware of the Devil and his

schemes? How would this knowledge aid us in our battle against demonic forces?

_____

_____

_____

_____

For more information on demons and how we should oppose them, turn to part 2 of this study guide and read chapter 10: "Identifying Demons."

INVASION OF DEMONS

The fourth and lowest position in Satan's realm is held by the "hosts of wickedness" (Ephesians 6:12), most commonly known as demons. They are the foot soldiers of his evil army and are dominated and directed by the higher-ranking rulers, powers, and principalities.

1. Look up the words *Devil* and *demon* in a dictionary. Write out the definitions below:

- Devil

_____

- demon

_____

2. Based on these definitions, and the explanation in "Invasion of Demons" in chapter 5 of *The Three Heavens*, what is the difference between the Devil and his demons?

_____

_____

_____

_____

3. Read Luke 22:3. What did you learn about the Devil in this verse?

_____
_____
_____
_____

4. Read Luke 8:30, 33. What can demons do that the Devil cannot do?

_____
_____
_____
_____

5. We have learned that the Devil cannot physically possess a person. But he does try to counterfeit the supernatural influence that the Holy Spirit has in a Christian's life. What kind of evil influence can the Devil, with the assistance of his demons, have on someone who is not covered by the blood of Jesus? For examples, see Mark 5:1–13 and Acts 19:16.

_____
_____
_____
_____
_____

WHAT CHARACTERIZES DEMONS?
Like their leader, demons have personalities and purposes that define their objective.

1. Read the descriptions of demons in *The Three Heavens* ("What Characterizes Demons?") and make a list below of the twelve characteristics:

   1. _____
   2. _____
   3. _____
   4. _____
   5. _____
   6. _____
   7. _____
   8. _____
   9. _____
   10. _____
   11. _____
   12. _____

2. Which of these characteristics was surprising to you? Which ones seemed significant to you?

   _____
   _____
   _____
   _____
   _____
   _____
   _____
   _____

They [demons] will continue to torment and possess till Christ comes again to redeem His Church. Until then, we remain at war!

• QUESTIONS FOR GROUP DISCUSSION •

1. Have you ever experienced Satan trying to thwart God's plan in your own life or in the life of someone you love? How? What happened? Discuss your experience in the light of this statement: *When God establishes, Satan opposes.*

2. Discuss this statement: *We, like the angels and Adam and Eve before us, have been given the free will to choose between good and evil—between becoming servants of Christ or slaves to sin and Satan.* In what ways is free will a gift? What would it be like if God had not given us free will? What are the consequences—both positive and negative—of having free will?

3. Review what you learned this week about Satan and his Kingdom. Where is the Second Heaven, according to Scripture? Who lives there? What takes place there? What are the four levels of authority in Satan's Kingdom recorded in the Bible? What are the differences between the Devil and his demons? Scripturally support your answers. Discuss the insights you learned this week by reading chapter 10 of this study guide: "Identifying Demons."

PRAY

Heavenly Father, we praise You because You are sovereign over all, and You are mightier than Satan and any of his demons. Thank You that through the power of Jesus Christ and His Word, we can expel evil spirits. But most of all, thank You that Christ has already won the battle against evil at the Cross through His victory over death, hell, and the grave! We can walk in assurance, knowing that the victory is ours through Christ! In Jesus' name we pray. Amen.

ACTION POINTS

1. *Remember this truth: "Pride cannot live beneath the cross."*[5] *Pride is sin, and God cannot coexist with sin.* Look over your answers in the "Birth of a Rebel" section. Is there any root of pride in your life that you have not confessed? If so, confess and repent of it now!

2. Look up current news headlines about wars and bloodshed over the issue of religion today. Has your view about these stories changed as a result of your study this week? According to Scripture, who is ultimately behind this bloodshed?

3. Log on to your Internet browser and bookmark news sites such as the *Jerusalem Post* (www.jpost.com) or the Drudge Report to stay up-to-date on current events about religious strife around the world. To take action on a more practical level, subscribe to the CUFI (Christians United for Israel) Newsletter at www.cufi.org. CUFI will alert you regarding topics crucial to Jerusalem and the nation of Israel and will give you the opportunity to show your support in tangible ways that express your solidarity with Israel and the Jewish people.

4. When you consider the overwhelming impact of Satan and his Kingdom, are you tempted to be fearful of his power? If so, write down the various ways his influence concerns you.

Now take action against those fears by proclaiming the following verse out loud: "You are of God, little children, and have overcome them, because He who is in you is greater than he who is in the world" (1 John 4:4). Remember this important truth—the Spirit of God within you is infinitely greater than any power of Satan and his demons. Now cross out the fears you named as you say a prayer of thanksgiving to God for replacing your fear with faith.

Week 4
Invasion of Demons in Society and the Church

STUDY OF CHAPTERS 6–7 IN *THE THREE HEAVENS*

....

Man is drawn to the supernatural like a moth to a flame.
A divine spark in each of us senses something more
beyond our world. The question is, what?
—John Hagee, *The Three Heavens*

....

Prepare for Week 4

- Read chapter 6, "Invasion of Demons in Society," in *The Three Heavens.*
- Read chapter 7, "Invasion of Demons in the Church," in *The Three Heavens.*

KEY VERSE

Now the Spirit expressly says that in latter times
some will depart from the faith, giving heed to
deceiving spirits and doctrines of demons.

—1 TIMOTHY 4:1

KEY PASSAGE FROM *THE THREE HEAVENS*

It's been forty-four years since my first eye-opening experience with demonic forces. The more I researched these oppressive spirits, the more I recognized that their presence invades our daily lives and has a far more destructive effect on every aspect of our society than we can imagine.

—*The Three Heavens,* chapter 6

⚭

• QUESTIONS FOR PERSONAL STUDY •

CHAPTER 6: INVASION OF DEMONS IN SOCIETY

I was bewildered. She was bewitched! Here was a woman glorifying the Devil with passionate fervor, right in the pastor's study!

1. Read the story of the woman who came to Pastor Hagee's study, at the beginning of chapter 6 of *The Three Heavens*. If you were the pastor, how would you have responded to the woman's confession? Would you have believed her? Why or why not?

2. Note the woman's reaction to *a scriptural counterattack*. How did she respond to the Word of God? How did she respond to the name of Jesus? What does this tell you about the power of Satan versus the power of Jesus Christ?

3. Read Philippians 2:9–11. According to this passage, how do demons respond to the name of Jesus Christ? How does this correspond to the reaction of this woman when Pastor Hagee declared the name of Jesus Christ?

I believe every word of God's sacred Scripture, so I began to pray to the Lord for direction. I asked for wisdom (James 1:5) and discernment (Proverbs 3:1–3) and ventured the question, "Lord, why did You allow this to happen?"

4. Read Luke 8:26–33. What connections did you see between the demon-possessed man in Gadara and the woman who came into Pastor Hagee's study? From your observation of this Scripture passage, what effects can demons have when possessing a person who *does not* know Christ? What other facts about demons did you learn from reading this Bible passage?

_____

_____

_____

_____

INVASION OF THE HOME

Sadly, Bible truths are not what our society is planting in the fertile minds of our children. Yet in faithful accordance with the promise of the ancient proverb, our children will not *depart from what their young minds are taught, whether good or evil.*

1. Read Proverbs 22:6. What does it mean to "train up" a child? List the specific ways a parent can accomplish this.

_____

_____

_____

_____

2. What does Proverbs 22:6 mean by "in the way he should go"? What is "the way"? Read this verse in several different

Bible translations and then describe below any insights you gain.

_____

_____

_____

_____

3. In your opinion, why is it essential to train the minds of children while they are young, as opposed to waiting until they are older?

_____

_____

_____

_____

SATAN'S DAYCARE

I can assure you that our children, for the most part, will become what they behold. And what they have the opportunity to behold in today's media is alarming.

1. Consider this statement: *Many animated children's programs feature witches, warlocks, violence, and utter pandemonium.* Do you agree or disagree with that statement? Describe a few of today's children's television programs and movies. What examples of witchcraft, violence, and chaos can you observe in these shows? Be specific.

_____

_____

_____

_____

2. In what ways can Satan influence impressionable young minds? What would be the advantage to Satan of introducing the occult into young children's cartoons, toys, games, and books?

---

3. Proverbs 23:7 says, "As [a person] thinks in his heart, so is he." In what ways does Satan influence how people think through today's media, including television, movies, books, social media, the Internet, etc.? Give specific examples.

---

4. Have you or your children watched shows that feature witches, sorcery, casting spells, incantations, or other occult themes? If so, list them below. Commit today to stop allowing yourself or your family to watch or read things that glorify Satan and his demonic forces.

SATAN'S SIMULATORS

We are being manipulated and dominated by destructive manipulation.

1. Do you or your children play video games? If so, which games do you regularly play?

   _____

   _____

   _____

   _____

2. Do any of the games you play include violence, occult themes, or other adverse or suggestive themes? (Examples include *Grand Theft Auto, The Walking Dead,* etc.) If so, which ones?

   _____

   _____

   _____

   _____

3. Based on what you read in the "Satan's Simulators" section of *The Three Heavens,* what are some of the possible real-world effects of indulging in a virtual world of violence?

   _____

   _____

   _____

   _____

VIDEO GAME RATINGS

A good indicator of video games that may be excessively violent or include occult or suggestive themes is the rating: M for "mature" or A for "adult." According to the Entertainment Software Ratings Board (ESRB), "M" ratings are for content that "may contain intense violence, blood and gore, sexual content and/or strong language." "A" ratings "may include prolonged scenes of intense violence, graphic sexual content and/or gambling with real currency." The ESRB defines "intense violence" as "graphic and realistic-looking depictions of physical conflict. May involve extreme and/or realistic blood, gore, weapons and depictions of human injury and death."[1]

However, don't be misled even by this rating system because the most "innocent" of games can also lure you or your child into the grips of the underworld.

SATAN'S SYMPHONY

What kind of music is your child listening to? Are they songs with harmless messages or songs with blatantly subversive lyrics accompanied by alluring rhythms? The latter are composed by the Master Architect of Evil for the purpose of destroying our future generation.

1. Read Zephaniah 3:17; Judges 5:3; and Revelation 15:3. What did you learn from these Bible verses about God's attitude toward music? Who sings in these verses and what kinds of songs do they sing?

2. Give examples of music in the modern eras that were composed as *works of praise unto the Lord*. Name a few contemporary songs you can think of that praise and worship God.

_____

_____

_____

_____

_____

For everything that God created as good, however, Satan has devised a counterfeit for evil. Many of today's musical expressions include messages of sodomy, blasphemy, drugs, adultery, illicit sex, female degradation, suicide, and murder.

3. What examples of Satan's counterfeits have you observed in today's popular music? Think of the songs on current *Billboard* charts, the songs featured on the Grammy Awards, and so on. Name a few songs or musical artists who exemplify satanic influences in their music.

_____

_____

_____

_____

4. Does any of the music you or your children listen to include lyrics that glamorize illicit drug use, encourage demoralizing sexual activity, or blaspheme God? If so, which ones? Do

you consider these songs to be "harmless" because you "just like the beat"? Why or why not?

_____

_____

_____

_____

5. Have you ever been negatively influenced by any lyrics you have listened to (such as foul language, messages on promiscuity or drug usage, etc.)? In what ways did these lyrics affect you? Be specific.

_____

_____

_____

_____

6. Based on what you read in the "Satan's Symphony" section of *The Three Heavens*, what are some of the possible real-world effects of listening to demoralizing and godless music?

_____

_____

_____

Satan has successfully planned and is currently executing a full-frontal assault to capture the minds and souls of our children and our children's children. Meanwhile, our generation is apathetic or is blinded to the reality of Satan's demonic plot.

TOXIC TELEVISION

You would never allow a known murderer to walk through the front door of your home without putting a gun in his face to protect your family. However, too few parents hesitate to click a remote, and so they invite him into their family's mind and soul through their television set.

1. On an average day, how many hours of television do you and your family watch? How many hours per week?

    _____

    _____

    _____

2. Read Matthew 12:33. What does this verse reveal about the "fruit" of the things we plant in our hearts and minds?

    _____

    _____

    _____

3. Write out below a few of the television shows that you watch.

    _____

    _____

    _____

4. Looking at the list above, circle any shows that feature violence or depravity. Based on what you have read in the "Toxic Television" section, what decision will you make

moving forward regarding those shows? Write out your commitment below.

_____

_____

_____

_____

SATAN'S CINEMA

Could it be that we have become so accustomed to dark messages that we are insensitive to what this genre of movies represents? Most definitely!

1. Do you or your loved ones watch horror movies or movies about exorcisms, demons, or the occult? If so, list below a few of the movies you have seen surrounding these topics.

_____

_____

_____

2. Do you consider these kinds of movies harmless entertainment? Why or why not? What kind of effects could these movies have on your mind and spirit?

_____

_____

_____

_____

3. How did the information presented in the "Satan's Cinema" section affect your opinion of this genre of movies? What decision will you make today as a result of your understanding?

_____

_____

_____

_____

We must recognize that Satan craves control of the world. The battle rages for the minds of our future generations. There will be a winner and a loser in this war, and to the winner goes our children!

CHAPTER 7: INVASION OF DEMONS IN THE CHURCH

Church membership will not save you, denominations will not save you, ritual will not save you, and singing "Amazing Grace" at the top of your lungs will not save you. And by all means, sitting in church will not guarantee immunity from satanic attack. Salvation only comes through faith in Christ.

1. Read 1 Timothy 4:1. According to this verse, what will happen in the latter times?

_____

_____

_____

Let the Church understand this truth: we are at war with Satan and his Kingdom, and we will be until he is cast into the Lake of Fire by the Conqueror of Calvary, Jesus Christ our Lord!

2. Did our battle with Satan end at the cross of Jesus Christ? Why or why not? Support your answer.

_____

_____

_____

_____

THE DEVIL AND MRS. SMITH

She opened the conversation with these words: "Pastor Hagee, could you come pray for me? I think I have a demon!"

1. Read the story of Pastor Hagee's encounter with Mrs. Smith, "The Devil and Mrs. Smith" in chapter 7. How is Mrs. Smith described in this story? What can you learn from this story about the presence of demonic activity in seemingly normal lives?

_____

_____

_____

2. What did Mrs. Smith admit to be her connection to the occult? Have you ever played with a Ouija board? If so, describe your experience. Was this harmless fun? Why or why not?

_____

_____

_____

_____

TAROT CARDS

Tarot cards are a form of divination used to measure potential outcomes and evaluate influences surrounding a person or event. The Tarot is a deck of seventy-eight cards. Standard Tarot decks have two types of cards: Major and Minor Arcana. They are divided into four suits, with each suit having one card for 1 to 10, and then face cards referred to as the page, knight, queen and king. Each Tarot card carries a message common to humanity. Tarot readers claim to use these cards to connect to your energies and foretell your future.[2]

3. Read Isaiah 47:10–15. What warnings does the Lord give to those who choose to participate in forms of divination, such as a Ouija board or Tarot cards? How effective are these types of sorcery in accurately foretelling future events?

_____

_____

_____

The Lord was showing me that an invasion of demonic spirits can happen anywhere, not only in the far reaches of the world, as I had previously been taught. I discovered through this extraordinary episode with Mrs. Smith that these forces must be confronted and can only be defeated through spiritual warfare and the ultimate power of God's Word.

4. After reading the description of Mrs. Smith's demonic possession and exorcism in *The Three Heavens*, write out your

thoughts below. What were some of the physical manifestations of her demonic possession? How did Pastor Hagee confront this demon? What was her response? What was the final result? Discuss what you learned from this demonic encounter.

_____

_____

_____

_____

_____

THE SHOOTER

The man's spiteful voice resonated throughout the church as he counted: "One . . . two . . ." and then began shooting at us from point-blank range, no more than eight feet away.

Miraculously, every shot missed!

1. Read the account of this shooter's invasion of Pastor Hagee's church in chapter 7 of *The Three Heavens*.

2. Go to getv.org to view Pastor Hagee's sermon "Angels: To Protect and Defend." Listen to the audio recording of this shooter's attempt to kill Pastor Hagee and the church member. What was your reaction to Satan's blatant assault in the house of God?

_____

_____

_____

_____

3. Read Psalm 34:7; Psalm 121:7; and Isaiah 54:17. What did you learn from these verses about God's protection of His children? How do these verses relate to the events that are described in the section "The Shooter" in *The Three Heavens*?

_____

_____

_____

_____

My message is simple: Satan and his demonic Kingdom truly exist, his power is real, and his objective is to destroy God's people.

THE EXORCIST COMES TO CHURCH

The mother told me that her daughter had gone to see The Exorcist *the week before. She then reported, "When my daughter returned home she told me, 'Something changed in me while I watched that movie. I feel different inside.'"*

1. Describe the young woman's sudden transformation, as detailed in *The Three Heavens*. What did she say happened to her while watching the movie?

_____

_____

_____

_____

2. To what did her mother attribute the young woman's sudden change in behavior? If your child had come home from watching a movie and told you, "Something changed

in me while I watched that movie," how would you have responded as her parent?

_____

_____

_____

3. Do you think a medical doctor or psychiatrist could fully address the young woman's torment? Why or why not?

_____

_____

WITCHCRAFT IN COSTA RICA

"Witchcraft rules our city. These spirits are strong and ruthless. Pastor, I am ashamed to say that I was afraid to admit or confront the fact that there were demonic forces in my home."

1. Have you ever traveled outside the United States and encountered a culture influenced by sorcery and witchcraft? If so, describe your experience.

_____

_____

2. When reading the story of the demon-possessed Costa Rican woman in *The Three Heavens*, were you surprised to learn that the woman was the wife of a local pastor? If so, why is this surprising? What would you have done if you were in the place of the pastor? Would you have confronted

the demonic spirit in your spouse, or would you have tried to conceal it to keep up appearances or avoid giving your ministry a negative reputation?

_____

_____

_____

3. This woman is described as *living in spiritual slavery in a church that was simply failing to teach the words and actions of Jesus Christ in dealing with evil spirits.* If your church does not teach on how to deal with evil spirits, I highly recommend you read works by Derek Prince on this subject by going to derekprince.org.

_____

_____

_____

THE KACHINA DOLL

This Christian family unknowingly opened the door to evil when they purchased these "dolls" to adorn their dwelling. Remember this truth: Satan is the great Deceiver; he will tempt you with items that look, feel, or sound appealing. He knows that, if and when you allow these objects entrance into your home, the wickedness they represent will infect your entire family.

1. Look up *Kachina* in a dictionary. Write out the definition below.

_____

_____

_____

2. If your dictionary didn't include a picture of a Kachina doll, look up a picture online. Do you recognize the Kachina doll, either from your own collection or from a friend's house or perhaps a place where you have shopped?

_____

_____

_____

_____

3. Based on what you read in "The Kachina Doll" section of *The Three Heavens*, how would you respond to someone who has a Kachina doll in his or her home and claims, "It's just for decoration. It doesn't mean anything"? Is it truly harmless to collect this type of statue or artwork? Discuss.

_____

_____

_____

4. Read Psalm 97:7 and Isaiah 2:8. How do these verses relate to collecting carved idols for decoration?

_____

_____

_____

• QUESTIONS FOR GROUP DISCUSSION •

1. If you are a parent, are you training your children in the way they should go (Proverbs 22:6)? If so, how? If not, what

practices can you start today to train them in the ways of the Lord? What other children are under your influence and example? (Perhaps in the church nursery, in a classroom, grandchildren, nieces and nephews, etc.) How can you begin to influence these children in the way they should go? In what ways can your group be a positive influence? Discuss specific strategies.

2. Read and discuss the following statement: *It is a fact that when you open your mind to a demonic force, you are in very real danger of being invaded by that spirit emotionally, physically, and spiritually. Be careful what you allow your children to watch—they will become what they behold, and not every movie has a happy ending!* Based on what you have learned in this chapter, what are some examples of ways you could "open your mind" to a demonic force? Be specific. What is the difference between being possessed by a demon and being influenced by demonic forces? Do you think Christians are immune to Satan's temptations and influence? Why or why not?

3. What did you learn in your study this week about demon possession? What does demonic possession look like? Who does it affect? What should we do when we encounter someone who has been strongly influenced by or actually possessed by a demonic spirit? How can demonic influence and possession be prevented? How would you respond, based on the Bible, to someone who is demon possessed? Discuss any insights you learned from reading chapter 11 of this study guide: "Expelling Demons."

Pray

Heavenly Father, we choose to live today—and every day—in the light of Your truth. Show us the ways we have given the Devil a foothold in our minds and hearts. Help us to walk on the path to deliverance and freedom, for Your Word declares that if the Son makes us free, we shall be free indeed. Give us the strength to stay focused on living the abundant life of the believer free of demonic influence. In the name of our one and only Savior and Redeemer we pray. Amen.

Action Points

1. Are you being influenced by Satan in any of your media consumption? Think about all the books, games, television shows, movies, YouTube videos, websites, and social media you view on a regular basis. Do any of these include aspects of the occult, such as witchcraft, casting spells, vampires, sorcery, and the like? If so, confess your involvement in the occult to the Lord right now. Write out your commitment that you will never again give the Devil a foothold in your life by watching or reading these things.

2. What objects are in your possession that may be influenced by the occult? Do you collect statues or artwork of dubious origin? Take a close look around your home and be aware of the history behind the objects you collect or display. Search your home with a new set of eyes. If you own anything with a demonic or occultic connection, remove it now!

Week 5
Evil and the Antichrist

STUDY OF CHAPTERS 8–9 IN *THE THREE HEAVENS*

What you see, you think on! Your thoughts
will become your speech, and your speech eventually
will become your actions. What you behold, you become!
The evil you allow into your mind can overpower you
and ultimately destroy you and others.

—John Hagee, *The Three Heavens*

Prepare for Week 5

- Read chapter 8, "The Evolution of Evil," in *The Three Heavens*.
- Read chapter 9, "The Spirit of the Antichrist," in *The Three Heavens*.

KEY VERSE

There shall not be found among you anyone who makes
his son or his daughter pass through the fire, or one
who practices witchcraft, or a soothsayer, or one who
interprets omens, or a sorcerer, or one who conjures spells,
or a medium, or a spiritist, or one who calls up the dead.
For all who do these things are an abomination to
the LORD, and because of these abominations
the LORD your God drives them out from before you.

—DEUTERONOMY 18:10–12

KEY PASSAGE FROM *THE THREE HEAVENS*

We have invited demonic forces into our society through a series of wide-open gates, and evil has gladly walked in. Satan has raped the minds, hearts, and souls of our young and indoctrinated them through his form of entertainment. . . .

The end result is the rejection of God Almighty and the acceptance of the devil, witchcraft, and all the evils of the occult. This highly calculated, well-executed, and very seductive campaign will pay off for the Evil One when those he has evangelized into the Kingdom of Darkness bow their knee and worship his son, the son of perdition known as the Antichrist.

—The Three Heavens, chapter 8

• QUESTIONS FOR PERSONAL STUDY •

CHAPTER 8: THE EVOLUTION OF EVIL

One would think that the toys, video games, books, music, and movies I cited in the previous chapters were destructive and heinous enough. However, the evolution of evil in our society through these various gateways has reached horrific levels.

DEVIL'S GATE

1. Do you believe that a Ouija board is a harmless board game, like Monopoly or Scrabble? Why or why not?

_____

_____

_____

_____

OUIJA BOARD

The 2014 horror film *Ouija* renewed popular interest in using the Ouija board, also known as a witch board or spirit board. The board is printed with letters and numbers, while a heart-shaped device slides over the board and supposedly contacts the dead. Playing with Ouija boards can lead to demonic possession. The Bible is clear that necromancy—the attempt to communicate with people who have died—is an abomination in the eyes of God (Leviticus 19:26; Deuteronomy 18:10; Galatians 5:19–20; Acts 19:19).[1]

2. Consider this comparison: *Becoming involved yourself with them [Ouija boards] is like leaving the gate to your home wide open in the middle of the night in a neighborhood with a sexual assault and murder rate that is the highest in the nation, hoping no evil monster will enter your home to murder or rape you. Your open gate is the Devil's invitation to enter.* Do you agree or disagree with this statement? Why?

_____
_____
_____
_____

3. Read the personal accounts of several young people who used Ouija boards in "Devil's Gate," chapter 8 of *The Three Heavens*. Do these factual accounts affect in any way your view of using a Ouija board—and other occult toys and games? If so, how?

_____
_____
_____
_____
_____

4. Read 1 Samuel 28:3–20. What did Saul do in this passage? Why? How did this affect Saul?

_____
_____
_____
_____

5. Do you think the spirit who spoke to Saul in 1 Samuel 28:15 was actually Samuel, God's prophet?

_____

_____

_____

_____

6. Read 1 Chronicles 10:13–14. What happened to Saul as a result of his disobedience to God in consulting a medium? What does this tell you about God's attitude toward divination, sorcery, and attempts to contact the dead?

_____

_____

_____

THE PROGRESSION OF EVIL

During my study for this book, I was astonished to observe the progression of evil within various areas of the entertainment industry in the past four decades.

1. Do an Internet search for the current "Top Ten Television Shows" and list them below. In light of what you have learned about Satan's influence through the media, what can you conclude about the themes associated with these programs?

_____

_____

_____

2. Now do an Internet search for the current "Top Ten Songs" and list them below. View the music videos that accompany the songs. What demonic themes or activities within the lyrics do you hear or see being presented? How do you think these songs and music videos are influencing today's youth?

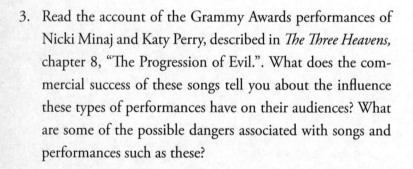

3. Read the account of the Grammy Awards performances of Nicki Minaj and Katy Perry, described in *The Three Heavens*, chapter 8, "The Progression of Evil.". What does the commercial success of these songs tell you about the influence these types of performances have on their audiences? What are some of the possible dangers associated with songs and performances such as these?

4. What were some of the real-world consequences of the violent movies *Natural-Born Killers*, *The Basketball Diaries*, and

The Matrix? Write out some of the associated murders beside each movie title.

- *Natural-Born Killers*

- *The Basketball Diaries*

- *The Matrix*

5. Based on your observations in question #4 above, are there any changes you need to make to the kinds of movies you or your children choose to watch?

DARKNESS RISES

Even this secular psychologist, who isn't trained to give credibility to spiritual matters, understands far too well the evil that is being celebrated in our culture.

1. Describe the events that took place in Aurora, Colorado, on July 20, 2012 at the movie theater premiering the film *The Dark Knight Rises.* Do you remember the news accounts of this incident? If so, what was your reaction to hearing of this murderous shooting rampage?

2. In what ways did the movie theater shooting in Aurora, Colorado, bear similarities to a scene in the 1986 comic book *Batman: The Dark Knight Returns?* (Discussed in "Darkness Rises," chapter 8 in *The Three Heavens.*)

_____

_____

_____

_____

_____

3. Do you observe any connection between reading the 1986 comic book and the subsequent 2012 shooting? What does this tell you about the demonic influence that seemingly harmless comic books can have in real life?

_____

_____

_____

_____

Author's update: James Holmes, the shooter who executed this deadly rampage, was found guilty of twelve counts of murder and wounding seventy others and is currently serving a life sentence in the Colorado State Penitentiary.

RIGHTEOUSNESS VERSUS LAWLESSNESS
Know this truth: There exists good and evil, light and darkness, truth and deception. The movie The Dark Knight Rises *was driven by the spirit of darkness.*

1. Read Colossians 1:13. How would you define "the power of darkness" based on what you have read so far?

_____

_____

_____

_____

2. Read 2 Corinthians 6:14. How are we as Christians to relate to things that are based in darkness?

_____

_____

_____

3. How does Jesus describe the church in Matthew 5:14? How does this description contrast with Satan's Kingdom?

_____

_____

_____

_____

4. Read the verse below out loud and answer the following questions.

For the weapons of our warfare are not carnal but mighty in God for pulling down strongholds, casing down arguments and every high thing that exalts itself against the knowledge of God, bringing every thought into captivity to the obedience of Christ. (2 Corinthians 10:4–5)

In what specific ways can you bring "every thought into captivity to the obedience of Christ"? What does this verse tell you about the importance of our private thoughts?

_____

_____

_____

_____

_____

"BRINGING EVERY THOUGHT INTO CAPTIVITY"

The phrase "bringing every thought into captivity" comes from a military term that meant to take captive as a prisoner or be led away captive (Luke 21:24). In Romans 7:23 Paul uses this term to describe the power of sin to make us a spiritual prisoner. In 2 Corinthians 10:5, *aichmalotizo* means to take control of all our thoughts, subjecting them to Christ. The present tense calls for this action to be our habitual practice, because we live in a world ruled by our enemy, the Devil, and we are constantly being bombarded with his fiery missiles in the form of the things we think about.[2]

CHAPTER 9: THE SPIRIT OF THE ANTICHRIST

If one opposes Jesus Christ and His Kingdom, the same is influenced by the "spirit of the Antichrist." This spirit personifies lawlessness and rebellion against delegated authority and defies all that Christ is: His Word, His virgin birth, and His death and resurrection.

1. Read 2 John 1:7. What does this verse say about those who possess an "antichrist" spirit?

_____

_____

_____

2. Read Matthew 24:5, 24; Mark 13:22; 1 John 2:18; 2:22; 4:1, 3; and 2 John 7. Write below how these verses confirm that there is one Antichrist and many "antichrists."

_____

_____

_____

3. Read Daniel 7:7, 25 and Revelation 13:3, 14; 17:1–15. Describe below what you learned from these verses about the person known as the Antichrist and the Great Harlot (or the Apostate Church, which is the counterfeit to the Bride of Christ).

_____

_____

_____

4. Read 2 Thessalonians 2:8–12. What title is used for the Antichrist in this passage? What will the coming Antichrist

be like? What will he do? How will the people respond to him?

_____

_____

_____

_____

THE CHURCH OF SATAN
The Church of Satan is the antithesis of the Church of Jesus Christ.

1. Read "The Church of Satan" section in *The Three Heavens*. In the space provided below, answer the following questions regarding the origins and effects of the Church of Satan:

*   Who founded the Church of Satan?

    _____

    _____

*   What are some of its rituals?

    _____

    _____

*   In what ways are these rituals counterfeits (or the antithesis) of rituals within the Christian church?

    _____

    _____

    _____

- What did you learn from this section regarding Satan's goal to replace God?

_____

_____

_____

MARKETING THE PRINCE OF DARKNESS

Satanists have hijacked our nation's sacred freedoms and use them to promote themselves, their beliefs, and their leader, the Prince of Darkness.

1. What did you learn from reading the "Marketing the Prince of Darkness" section in *The Three Heavens* about recent attempts by the Church of Satan to exploit First Amendment rights and be recognized as a legitimate religion in America?

_____

_____

_____

_____

The Church of Satan's incessant efforts to legitimize itself as an accepted part of American society will continue until the Antichrist himself makes his appearance as the global dictator of Planet Earth. Let us not be deceived but be courageous in our constant battle for truth and righteousness as defined in the Word of God.

SATANIC RITUALS

The Church of Satan and its anti-God, anti-Christ philosophy has made a gruesome impact on our society, harvesting evil results.

1. Genesis 1:27 tells us that mankind is made "in the image of God." How do these satanic rituals defile God's creation?

_____

_____

_____

_____

UNHOLY PURSUITS

This death-worshiping spirit did not begin with the Church of Satan and satanic rituals. The spirit of the Antichrist has raised its atrocious head throughout history.

1. From your readings in *The Three Heavens* (chapter 9), write out below a short description of how each of the following people demonstrated the spirit of the antichrist:

- Cain (Genesis 4)

_____

- Abimelech (Judges 9)

_____

- Herod the Great (Matthew 2:16)

_____

- Herod Antipas (Matthew 14:6–11)

_____

- Nero

_____

_____

- Joseph Stalin

- Mao Tse-Tung

- Adolf Hitler

WHY DOES SATAN HATE
THE JEWISH PEOPLE?

In Genesis 12:3, God made an everlasting covenant with Abraham: "I will bless those who bless you, and I will curse him who curses you; and in you all the families of the earth shall be blessed." Israel is the only nation in the history of the world created by a sovereign act of God (Genesis 13:14–15; 17:7–8).

Every person reading this study guide has been blessed by the contributions of the Jewish people. The Jewish people have given us the Bible, the patriarchs, and the apostles. Most importantly, the Jewish people gave us our Lord and Savior, Jesus Christ. Christianity cannot explain its existence without Judaism. That's why our faith is referred to as the *Judeo-Christian faith*. Our roots are found in Abraham, Isaac, and Jacob.

God not only had a plan for the Jewish people that resulted in the birth of Jesus Christ and Christianity, but He has a future plan for the nation of Israel. Look at God's message to the Jewish people in Ezekiel 39: "'I will bring back the captives of Jacob, and have mercy on the whole house of Israel; and I will be jealous for My holy name. . . . I will not hide My face from them anymore; for I shall have poured out My Spirit on the house of Israel,' says the Lord GOD" (vv. 25, 29). What is the future for Israel? Mercy! What is God's plan for Israel? Deliverance!

So why does Satan hate the Jewish people? Because God has sworn to defend Israel, and Satan does everything he can to thwart God's plan. But do not fear: the Jewish people are still the apple of God's eye. They are still the chosen people. As God delivered them from Pharaoh . . . as He delivered them from Haman's plot . . . God will deliver them again. The God of Abraham, Isaac, and Jacob will continue to fight for Israel's defense![3]

2. Why does the Devil have such a deep-seated hatred for the Jewish people? How does God describe Himself in Psalm 121:4? How do you see God's sovereignty demonstrated in the fact that the Jewish people have survived?

HITLER AND THE OCCULT

One should not underestimate the influence of the occult on Hitler. The root of Hitler's lust for godlike status, his drive for world power, and his twisted philosophies of self-indulgence and anti-Semitism were born of Satan himself.

1. What did you learn about Adolf Hitler from reading the "Hitler and the Occult" section in *The Three Heavens*?

_____

_____

_____

2. In what ways was Hitler influenced by Dietrich Eckart? What was Eckart's connection to the occult? Why do you think this is significant?

_____

_____

_____

3. Do you think that Hitler's desire for godlike status, combined with his incredible capability of mesmerizing a large audience with his ranting discourse, reveal that he was being influenced by Satan?

_____

_____

_____

RADICALIZED OR DEMONIZED

As Christ represents life, the Antichrist spirit represents death. Fanatical extremism has been responsible for a countless number of killings throughout history. This psychopathic, amoral ideal will exist until the return of the Messiah.

1. When you hear the term "radicalized extremists," what kinds of images come to your mind?

_____

_____

_____

_____

2. Look up the word *radicalized* in the dictionary and write out the definition below.

_____

_____

_____

3. Radicalized terrorist organizations include Al Qaeda, the Taliban, and ISIS (also called ISI and ISIL, or the Islamic State). What are some recent examples of actions taken by these radicalized terrorists? Why do you think these groups employ such violent extremism?

_____

_____

_____

_____

_____

THE WILL AND THE POWER

The startling truth of today is that in less than fifteen years after 9/11, radicalized jihadists not only possess the will *to destroy Israel, America, and the West but the financial* power *to do so!*

1. What is your response to reading about the rise of the Islamic State in "The Will and the Power" section in *The Three Heavens*?

_____

_____

_____

_____

_____

2. What did you learn about the power and influence that this radicalized group exerts over the entire world? What did you learn about the Islamic State's attitude toward Christians and Jews?

_____

_____

_____

_____

3. As we wrap up this week's study, read aloud the following Scripture passage. Then write out what you learned from this passage about what we can do in response to the forms of evil we observe in the world around us.

Finally, my brethren, be strong in the Lord and in the power of His might. Put on the whole armor of God, that you may be able to stand against the wiles of the devil. For we do not wrestle against flesh and blood, but against principalities, against powers, against the rulers of the darkness of this age, against spiritual hosts of wickedness in the heavenly places.

Therefore take up the whole armor of God, that you may be able to withstand in the evil day, and having done all, to stand. (Ephesians 6:10–13)

• QUESTIONS FOR GROUP DISCUSSION •

1. As you studied this week, how did you feel when you became more conscious of the fact that "the spirit of the Antichrist" is rapidly increasing? Do you see any connection between current events and the signs of the coming Antichrist? What could it mean for our generation? What "signs of the times" can we currently observe in our own world?

2. Discuss the following statement: *The demonized, radical, megalomaniacs discussed in this chapter were and are obsessed with total power at all costs, just like their Evil Mentor, who has come to rob, kill, and destroy (John 10:10). The devastation they have left in their wake has already cost multiple millions of innocent lives—and the numbers are only rising.* What similarities did you see in this chapter between various demon-influenced individuals and the Devil himself? What did you learn about Satan's ultimate goal for mankind? How has this chapter shaped your understanding of current world events? In what way can we protect ourselves from Satan and his schemes?

3. Read Ephesians 6:14–17. Notice that each part of the armor corresponds to spiritual attitudes that the believer must maintain. The armor protects; however, it does not substitute for the actions in warfare we should take against the enemy.

- *Girdle of Truth*—The girdle of truth represents the clear understanding of God's Word, which is absolute truth. It is very much like a belt that keeps the rest of the armor in place.
- *Breastplate of Righteousness*—The breastplate of righteousness protects the heart of the believer and is reflected in our obedience to the Word by which we receive God's blessings.
- *Feet Shod with the Gospel of Peace*—Having our feet shod with the gospel of peace is the foundation that every believer stands on, Christ our Savior. It reflects our faithful proclamation of the Gospel given through our testimony and by our deeds.
- *Shield of Faith*—The shield of faith covers all the other parts of the armor; it is our salvation and our protection. Our belief in Christ protects us from the attacks of the Evil One. Our faith in our Redeemer will overcome the world.
- *Helmet of Salvation,* also the Hope of Salvation (1 Thessalonians 5:8)—The helmet of salvation protects the mind from the arrows of the enemy. It is our confidence in the coming of the Lord, which is our ultimate redemption.

- *Sword of the Spirit*—The sword of the Spirit is the Word of God. We proclaim His Word in every battle producing every victory; it is the only offensive weapon we have—all else is defense.

4. What does it mean to put on the whole armor of God? How would that affect your daily life—your thoughts, your actions, your leisure time, etc.? Discuss specific ways you and your group can encourage one another to put on the armor of God daily.

PRAY

Heavenly Father, Your Word is truth. We ask for Your discernment that helps us to separate ourselves from the world and draw closer to You. Please open our eyes and hearts to what You require of us. Help us to walk confidently in obedience to Your Word, taking every thought captive. Give us the wisdom and the strength to put on Your armor, which protects us from the destructive plans of the Evil One. We ask and receive in the mighty name of Jesus. Amen.

ACTION POINTS

1. If you have a Ouija board or Tarot cards or anything in your home connected to the occult, remove it now!

2. Commit to bring "every thought into captivity to the obedience of Christ" (2 Corinthians 10:5). Begin by writing down the things you need to stop listening to or watching. Then create another list of ways you can build up your faith

(Jude 20). One way is to memorize one verse of Scripture each week and meditate on His Word.

3. Ephesians 6:18 tells us to pray for the saints without ceasing. Through our supplication and thanksgiving we stay in the presence of God. Ask your study group to commit to daily prayer. Remember, Jesus promises us, "Where two or three are gathered together in My name, I am there in the midst of them" (Matthew 18:20).

Week 6
Deliver Us from the Evil One

STUDY OF CHAPTER 10 IN *THE THREE HEAVENSS*

....

Satan's agenda is prospering on all fronts.
Every form of wickedness is escalating.
Our world is filled with bedlam, terrorism, murder,
blasphemy, depravity, deception, and occult activity.
—John Hagee, *The Three Heavens*

....

Prepare for Week 6

- Read chapter 10, "Deliver Us from the Evil One," in *The Three Heavens*.

Key Verse

I call heaven and earth as witnesses today against you,
that I have set before you life and death, blessing and cursing;
therefore choose life, that both you and your descendants
my live; that you may love the LORD your God,
that you may obey His voice, and that you may cling to Him,
for He is your life and the length of your days.
—Deuteronomy 30:19–20

Key Passage from *The Three Heavens*

The Church of Jesus Christ can no longer ignore this diabolical presence in our society. It is time to remove the veil of deception that has blinded us to satanic influence for far too long. We are called to be Christlike by following the examples that the Lord set before us (1 Peter 2:21–25). Like Christ, we must take a bold and fearless stand against the Prince of Darkness!

—*The Three Heavens*, chapter 10

☙

• Questions for Personal Study •

Chapter 10: Deliver Us from the Evil One

As I prayed, the Lord brought to my mind a very special memory that once again anchored me in the promise that no matter how dark the evil becomes, Jesus Christ is the Light who causes darkness to flee!

EXPELLING DEMONS

Looking over my congregation, I witnessed a worldwide wrestling match taking place on the platform, twelve women screaming like fire trucks going to a five-alarm call, and the dearly departed running for the back door. It was a night to remember. I laughed out loud! Who said church was a boring place?

1. Have you ever participated in a "deliverance service"? If so, describe your experience.

_____

_____

_____

_____

_____

2. Imagine you were in the evening worship service hosted by Derek Prince and heard his announcement: *"If you or anyone with you does not believe in demon spirits, I ask you to leave the sanctuary at this time."* How would you have responded? Would you have left or stayed? Explain your answer.

_____

_____

_____

_____

For more information on what you can do when you encounter demonic influence, turn to part 2 of this study guide and read chapter 11: "Expelling Demons."

SETTING THE CAPTIVES FREE

It is now time to take the next step and learn from Scripture how believers can be free from the Deceiver's attempts to influence our lives, our families, and our nation.

1. One of the first biblical accounts of Jesus' deliverance ministry is Luke 4:33–37. Read this passage and write out below what you observe about this episode.

_____

_____

_____

_____

2. Where did this expulsion of a demon take place? (See Luke 4:33.) What significance did you observe about the location of this exorcism?

_____

_____

_____

3. Read Luke 4:38–41. What did Jesus do immediately after expelling the demon from the man in the synagogue? What can you observe from this about Jesus' deliverance ministry?

_____

_____

_____

The Gates of Evil

Just as we must recognize and obey traffic signals to safely arrive at our destination, we must recognize the warning signals that God clearly defines in His Word to avoid the Devil's entrapments.

1. Have you ever thought the following: *"I don't listen to satanic music, I don't play with Ouija boards or hold séances, I don't watch horror movies or read occultic books, and I don't ascribe to Antichrist doctrines or seek world domination . . . so I don't need to worry about deliverance"*?

2. If you answered yes, what is the danger in believing you are beyond the reach of Satan's influence and temptations? (See 1 Corinthians 10:12.)

_____

_____

_____

The Mind Gate

Make no mistake: the battleground is the mind! Among the weapons of war used by Satan's demonic forces to attack your thoughts are doubt, confusion, indecision, compromise, humanism, and excessive fear or worry.

1. Read Genesis 3:4, 13; John 8:44; 2 Corinthians 11:3; 1 Thessalonians 3:5; and Revelation 12:9, 15. What did you learn from these verses about Satan's calculating plans?

_____

_____

_____

2. Consider this observation: *The people most vulnerable to these types of demonic assaults are those who rely on their own intellect rather than those who have faith in God's Word to take them through the storms of life.* Are you someone who relies on personal knowledge and experience when you are facing a problem or do you trust in God's Word for the solution?

_____

_____

_____

_____

3. Read Philippians 4:8 and then make a list of the eight things the apostle Paul instructs us to "think on":

- • _____
- • _____
- • _____
- • _____
- • _____
- • _____
- • _____

4. Ask yourself, "Where is my thought life leading me?" Write out your response below. What changes do you need to make in your thought life to conform to Christ?

_____

_____

_____

_____

_____

THE EMOTION GATE

Extreme negative emotions or destructive attitudes potentially open the gate for an equivalent spirit to come into your life.

1. What emotions do you tend to struggle with? (Examples include fear, worry, anxiety, sadness, hopelessness, etc.) How do you deal with these negative emotions?

    _____

    _____

    _____

    _____

    _____

2. We all struggle with certain emotions from time to time. But when these negative feelings dominate your everyday life, you need *to recognize them as a demonic attack, reject them in the authority of Jesus' name, and separate yourself from them.* Read through the following examples in the section "The Emotion Gate" in chapter 10 of *The Three Heavens* and then write below what you learned about how to deal with each of the following negative emotions:

*   Doubt—Matthew 17:20; Mark 11:23

    _____

*   Worry —Matthew 6:25–33: Luke 12:11, 22; Philippians 4:6; 1 Peter 5:7

    _____

*   Fear —Deuteronomy 20:1; 31:6; Joshua 1:9; Psalm 27:1; Isaiah 41:10, 13–14; 43:2, 5; Romans 8:31

    _____

- Resentment—Psalms 17; 27; 35; 109; 143)

THE SPEECH GATE

The presence of demonic influence can also be reflected in the content of a person's speech, such as compulsive lying, gossip, vulgar language, and destructive declarations.

1. Read James 3:6 and Proverbs 18:21. What do these verses tell us about the power of the tongue (our speech)?

2. What does God's Word exhort us to do? (See Psalm 34:13; Proverbs 13:3)

3. Read Psalm 101:5; Proverbs 16:28; and Romans 1:29–32. What did you learn from these verses about God's attitude toward deceit and lying?

4. Read Matthew 12:34–35. What connection did you observe from this passage between our speech and our heart? What does your typical pattern of speech reveal about you?

5. What does 1 Timothy 6:3–5 teach you about the effects of negative words? What are we commanded to do in respect to people who engage regularly in this type of speech?

6. What are we instructed to do in Colossians 3:8–10 to ensure we stay away from any malice or strife in our speech?

THE CARNAL GATE
Christians are commanded to be in control of their physical habits.

1. Read Romans 8:6. What is the result of being "carnally minded"?

CARNAL

The Greek word for *carnal* (*sarkikos*) means to have the characteristics of the flesh. This word is translated in the New Testament as "carnal," "earthly," or "fleshly."

What does the Bible mean by "the flesh"? The flesh refers to our sin nature. One Bible scholar says the flesh is "characterized by our natural desires and passions (Galatians 5:19–24; 1 John 2:16); it can enslave us (Romans 7:25); and in it is nothing good (Romans 7:18). Based on this meaning of the word *flesh*, to be "carnal" means to be characterized by things that belong to the unsaved life (Ephesians 2:3)."[1]

2. Take an inventory of any negative habits related to your carnal pleasures or desires. (Examples include compulsive eating, excessive alcohol consumption, pornography, extra-marital affairs, etc.) Write them out below.

_____

_____

_____

_____

_____

_____

3. Look at your list and answer the following question: "Does God want this for my life, or have I chosen a poison that will eventually destroy me?" Pay attention to these destructive habits! Ignoring them will lead to certain ruin. Remember; God cannot change what you will not confront!

4. Read 1 Corinthians 6:19–20. How has this passage enlightened you about your physical body? What are some ways you can "glorify God in your body?" (See Philippians 1:20.)

_____

_____

_____

_____

5. Read 2 Peter 1:3–11 and 1 Corinthians 15:57. How do these passages challenge you to be more diligent in your Christian walk? How do they encourage you? What lifestyle changes will you commit to making in light of these Bible promises?

_____

_____

_____

_____

Let every discouraged heart, every worried and tormented mind, every depressed and defeated spirit, cry out: there is deliverance in Jesus Christ!

RECOGNIZE, REJECT, AND REMOVE
Once we have recognized *the Evil Intruder, we must* reject *his influence and* remove *ourselves from his presence.*

1. Read the quote from Derek Prince in "Recognize, Reject, and Remove" in chapter 10 of *The Three Heavens*. Do you

believe that Christians are immune from demonic influence? What does Derek state about our vulnerability to the wiles of the Devil?

_____

_____

_____

_____

2. Read Luke 4:18. According to Jesus, who has the power to defeat Satan?

_____

_____

_____

3. Read Mark 16:17; Luke 10:17; and Acts 16:18. What did you conclude from these verses about believers' authority to cast out demons? How is this authority connected to your answer above?

_____

_____

_____

_____

Believers have both the authorization and the ability to be victorious over the powers and principalities of the Devil.

THE JOURNEY TO FREEDOM
Allow me to guide you on the same journey to freedom that Derek Prince first led my congregation on some forty years ago.

1. Read "The Journey to Freedom" section in *The Three Heavens* and circle or underline in the text of the book each of the seven suggested steps to deliverance offered in this section.

2. Now write out each of the steps provided:

    - _____
    - _____
    - _____
    - _____
    - _____
    - _____
    - _____

THE ACT OF DELIVERANCE

Once you have fulfilled each step, identify the enemy by name—whatever it is—reject it from your life, and then pray the prayer of deliverance, and the demon spirit that has held you hostage has no choice but to leave.

1. Read through the list above and ask yourself, "Have I gone through each of these steps to deliverance?" Put a check-mark beside the ones you have completed. Put a star beside the steps you still need to take to continue your journey to deliverance and spiritual freedom.

2. Realize that step 1 is the most important action of all. I have used the term "believer" throughout this study. Who is a believer? One who has confessed and repented of their sins and received Jesus Christ as their Savior and Lord. Take this time to accept Christ into your heart or rededicate your life

to Him. When this occurs the Lord will cover you with His shed blood and redeem you from eternal damnation.

3. Now that you have completed the steps, read the following deliverance prayer out loud:

Satan, in the name of Jesus and by the power of His shed blood I renounce you and your Kingdom. I reject your demon spirits of [call them by name] and their influence over my life. No longer will I be dominated by any stronghold that has held me captive. I receive my deliverancein the name of Jesus Christ. I am free! Amen. (See "The Act of Deliverance" in *The Three Heavens*.)

4. After you have spoken the prayer of deliverance, then celebrate your freedom! You are now liberated from the bondage sin. You have been renewed, restored, and redeemed. Give God all the glory for the victory!

PROTECTING YOUR FREEDOM
After you have experienced God's deliverance, it is imperative that you immerse yourself in His Word, attend a Bible-centered church that preaches the uncompromised gospel of Christ, and stay in fellowship with like-minded believers (Psalm 133:1; Philippians 1:5–6).

1. According to *The Three Heavens*, what two things must we do after we have been delivered from demonic influence?

    - _____
    - _____

2. Why do you think it is so important for a person who has been recently delivered from Satan's influence to fill his or her heart with the things of God? Read Luke 11:24–26 for insights.

_____

_____

_____

_____

You are in control of your destiny. Do not give Satan a foothold in your life that will steal your peace, your joy, and your hope. God promises to never leave or forsake us. He has presented His Word for our instruction, His Son for our redemption, and the Holy Spirit for our comfort and guidance.

• QUESTIONS FOR GROUP DISCUSSION •

1. Discuss this statement: *The Word of God, the name of Jesus, and the power of His blood have ultimate authority over any satanic attack.* How does the assurance of God's ultimate authority over Satan make you feel? How does this understanding affect the way you relate to the evil in this world? Discuss.

2. Look back at each of the four "gates" described in this chapter as opportunities for Satan to influence and torment you—the Mind Gate, the Emotion Gate, the Speech Gate, and the Carnal Gate. Have you opened a gate to Satan in your thoughts, emotions, words, or physical habits? What are the dangers of allowing the Devil to gain a foothold in any of these areas? Discuss.

3. What is the difference between *demon possession* and *demonic attack*? Discuss what you learned from this chapter about how to deal with a person who is demon possessed. Then review and discuss the seven steps to deliverance outlined in "The Journey to Freedom" section. If you have time, discuss any insights you learned this week by reading chapter 11 of this study guide: "Expelling Demons."

Pray

Heavenly Father, we thank You that through the power of Your Word and the power of the name and blood of Jesus Christ we can expel evil spirits from our midst. We pray for all those who are under demonic attack. We ask that You remove the scales of deception that have held them captive. Redeem them from the bondage of sin that has blinded them. Release them from the chains of addiction that have imprisoned them. We rejoice that Christ has already defeated Satan and his demons at the Cross! We declare that Jesus Christ has authority over every evil spirit and demonic influence in our lives and the lives of our loved ones. We give You all the praise and glory, for the victory is ours through Christ Jesus! Amen.

Action Point

1. The Bible urges us, "Examine yourselves as to whether you are in the faith" (2 Corinthians 13:5). Take a few moments to examine yourself and your heart. Have you accepted Jesus Christ as your Savior? Do you have the full assurance that you are covered with the blood of Jesus Christ, protecting you from demon possession and giving you the authority to cast out demons in His name?

Week 7
Where Angels Tread

STUDY OF CHAPTERS **11–12** IN *THE THREE HEAVENS*

I believe in God's angels, not because of a Renaissance artist's inspirational painting depicting winged cherubs playing harps while floating on fluffy white clouds; not because Hollywood has made mystical blockbuster movies on the subject; not because of someone's testimony of an angelic vision or because I have seen one (I have not).
I believe in angels because the Bible tells me they exist!
—John Hagee, *The Three Heavens*

Prepare for Week 7

- Read chapter 11, "Why I Believe in Angels," in *The Three Heavens*.
- Read chapter 12, "Where Angels Tread," in *The Three Heavens*.

KEY VERSE

To which of the angels did He ever say:
"You are My Son, today I have begotten You"?
And again: "I will be to Him a Father, and He shall be
to Me a Son"? But when He again brings the firstborn
into the world, He says: "Let all the angels of God
worship Him." And of the angels He says:
"Who makes His angels spirits and His minister a flame
of fire." . . . But to which of the angels has He ever said:
"Sit at My right hand, till I make Your enemies Your
footstool"? Are they not all ministering spirits sent
forth to minister for those who will inherit salvation?
—HEBREWS 1:5–7, 13–14

KEY PASSAGE FROM *THE THREE HEAVENS*

As children of God we are surrounded by an immeasurable, invisible, and invincible order of intelligent supernatural beings sent on a special mission by God Himself for our defense, our comfort, and our protection!

—*The Three Heavens*, chapter 11

• QUESTIONS FOR PERSONAL STUDY •

CHAPTER 11: WHY I BELIEVE IN ANGELS

I believe in angels because the Bible tells me they exist!

The Bible is the inerrant Word of God, and it is absolute *truth (John 17:17).*

WHAT ARE ANGELS?

To fully appreciate the reality of angels and their importance in a believer's life, one must first study the Holy Scriptures, which present detailed accounts of their existence, their characteristics, their office and ranks, their power to protect and defend and their assignments given by God Almighty.

1. What images come to your mind when you think of an angel? Write them out below.

_____

_____

_____

_____

_____

2. Now read the section "What Are Angels?" in *The Three Heavens*, chapter 11. Then write beside each Scripture reference the characteristic of angels you learn from that passage.
   - Colossians 1:16—
   - Psalm 104:4—
   - Genesis 19:1–3—
   - Mark 13:32; Revelation 10:1—

- Daniel 10:13; Hebrews 1:14—
- Psalm 103:20; 1 Peter 3:22; Jude 6—
- Ezekiel 1:1–5—
- Luke 20:34–35—
- Luke 2:10–11—
- Luke 2:13—
- Hebrews 1:6—
- 2 Peter 2:11; Jude 9—
- Luke 9:26; Revelation 14:10—
- Matthew 18:10—
- 1 Timothy 3:16—

3. According to Revelation 5:11, how many angels did God create? Where do they live?

_____

_____

_____

_____

ANGELIC CHARACTERISTICS

Angels are God's messengers who convey His commands and carry out His judgments; they perform God's bidding.

1. Read the section "Angelic Characteristics" in *The Three Heavens*. Then fill in the blanks below:
   - Angels are under _____ authority (1 Peter 3:22).
   - Angels' _____ and _____ are superior to those of man (Hebrews 2:7; 2 Samuel 14:20).

- Angels have supernatural _____ and _____ (2 Peter 2:11).
- Angels can _____ (Isaiah 6:6).
- Angels can _____ (Hebrews 2:2).
- Angels reflect God's _____ (Luke 15:10).
- Angels never _____ or _____ (Luke 20:35–36).
- Angels can discern between _____ and _____ (2 Samuel 14:17).
- Angels are our holy escorts in _____ and in _____ (Hebrews 1:14; Luke 16:22).
- Angels are without _____ (Daniel 7:10; Luke 2:13; Hebrews 12:22).

2. Based on what you have observed so far in the Bible's description of angels, in what ways has your mental image of them changed? Jot down a few of the new insights you have learned in your study of angels.

_____

_____

_____

_____

ANGELIC OFFICES
The office of an angel is fourfold.

1. In the space below, write out a short description of each of the following offices of angels.
- God's worshippers

_____

- God's ministers

- God's messengers

- God's agents

ANGELIC RANKS AND ASSIGNMENTS

Angels are organized in terms of authority, power, and glory. Their ranks consist of archangel, seraphim, cherubim, principalities, power, thrones, and dominion (Ephesians 1:21; Colossians 1:16; 1 Peter 3:22).

THE ANGEL OF THE LORD

1. Who is "the Angel of the Lord" or "the Angel of God"? Support your answer with Scripture. (See, for example, Genesis 32:24–30; 48:16; Exodus 23:20–23.)

2. What encouragement can you gain from the Angel of the Lord's appearance to Hagar, the mother of Ishmael, who was cast out of the house by Abraham's jealous wife? (See Genesis 21:17–19.)

3. Write out below any insight you gain about the Angel of the Lord from His appearances to the following people, as recorded in the Old Testament:
- Moses (Exodus 3:2)

_____

- Gideon (Judges 6:12)

_____

- Samson's mother (Judges 13:6)

_____

- Balaam (Numbers 22:31)

_____

THE ARCHANGEL

1. What is the name of the angel directly associated with the title "archangel"? (See Jude 9.)

_____

_____

2. Read Daniel 12:1. According to this verse, what is the Archangel's primary task?

_____

_____

3. Read Daniel 10:13, 21. What did you learn about Michael from these verses? What was his mission? Can any other angel succeed in overpowering him? (Go to Daniel 10:21).

_____

_____

_____

_____

4. How do the stories shared in the section "The Archangel" of *The Three Heavens* confirm Michael's ongoing protection of God's people, the children of Israel?

_____

_____

_____

_____

For more information on angels' ongoing ministry in the modern world, turn to part 2 of this study guide and read chapter 12: "The Elect Angels."

God's Special Messenger

1. Read Luke 1:19. What is the name of this angel, who holds the highest position of the angelic messengers?

_____

_____

2. God's personal emissary was sent by God at least four distinct times in Scripture. Write out your observations about Gabriel beside each of these four passages:

• Daniel 8:15–16

- Daniel 9:21–27

- Luke 1:11–20

- Luke 1:26–33

CHERUBIM

1. We have already read in Ezekiel 28:14, 16 that Lucifer was created as a cherub (plural: cherubim). Read Ezekiel's description of the cherubim in Ezekiel 1:4–28. Write out a few of their characteristics. Is this what you imagined a "cherub" to look like? How did Ezekiel respond to seeing these mighty angels? (v. 28).

2. Read Genesis 3:24. What assignment did God give to the cherubim in Eden? After reading Ezekiel's description of them in Ezekiel 1, does this change your mental image of angels "guarding" the Garden of Eden?

3. What four animals represent the four characteristics of cherubim, as described in Ezekiel 1:10?

- _____
- _____
- _____
- _____

SERAPHIM

1. How does Isaiah describe the seraphim that appeared to him? (Go to Isaiah 6:1–2.)

_____
_____
_____
_____

2. Read Isaiah 6:3. What is the assignment given to seraphim?

_____
_____
_____

3. Read Isaiah 6:4–7. How did the seraphim guard God's holiness and purify Isaiah from his sin? What correlation can you observe between this action and the meaning of the word *seraph* ("to burn")? What future, once-and-for-all purification does the live coal symbolize?

_____
_____
_____

CHAPTER 12: WHERE ANGELS TREAD

Angels are the servants of God. They heed His voice and carry out His mandates. They tread where He leads.

PETER'S ESCAPE

1. Read the Bible's account of *"the most famous jailbreak in the history of the world"* in Acts 12:7–11. In the space below, describe what the angel did to free Peter from his prison chains.

_____

_____

_____

2. Read Acts 12:15. How did the believers react to the young woman's news that Peter had been set free and was at the door? What can you infer from this about their belief in the power of angels?

_____

_____

_____

THE LIONS' DEN

1. Read Daniel 6:22–23. What did an angel do to protect Daniel? Why?

_____

_____

_____

2. How did the king respond to the angel's protection of Daniel (Daniel 6:23–26)?

_____

_____

_____

_____

THE CHARIOTS OF FIRE
Elijah's servant was terrified, but the prophet prayed that his servant could see what was revealed to him: angels sent by God to protect and deliver them.

1. Read 2 Kings 6:12–17. What did God reveal to Elijah's servant?

_____

_____

_____

_____

2. What did you learn from this verse about the ministry of angels to God's servants in protecting, defending, and guiding them?

_____

_____

_____

_____

THE INVINCIBLE SOLDIER
1. During the French and Indian War, George Washington was dubbed "The Invincible Soldier" because of God's

supernatural protection over him. Why do you think God's angels protected Washington during this war?

_____

_____

_____

_____

2. Read Psalm 91:11–12. How does this passage relate to the story of George Washington? Do you think this passage relates to your own life? Why or why not?

_____

_____

_____

THE FLAMING SWORDS

1. How did the raiding Mau Mau respond to the judge's question: "Why did you not complete the mission? Why didn't you attack the school?" (See "The Flaming Swords" in chapter 12 of *The Three Heavens*.)

_____

_____

_____

2. Based on what you have read so far in this chapter and in the Bible, how do you explain the *"huge men, dressed in glowing white with flaming swords"*? Who were they?

_____

_____

_____

3. Read Psalm 34:7. What did you learn about angels from this verse? What comfort can you take personally from this promise?

_____

_____

_____

_____

_____

GUARDIAN ANGELS

1. Read the section "Guardian Angels" in _The Three Heavens._ Have you ever experienced supernatural protection in a dangerous circumstance? If so, what happened? Do you think guardian angels played a role in your protection?

_____

_____

_____

_____

2. Read Matthew 18:10. What did you learn from this verse about guardian angels?

_____

_____

_____

_____

ANGELIC ESCORTS

When the righteous die, they are escorted from this life into the Third Heaven by angels, who take them to their mansions of splendor created by the Architect of the Ages (John 14:2).

1. Read Psalm 116:15 and Revelation 14:13. How does the Lord view the death of His saints? How did these verses encourage you about your own death or the death of a loved one?

_____

_____

_____

_____

2. What was your response to the stories in this section of believers who saw angels on their deathbed?

_____

_____

_____

_____

ANGELS ON THE BATTLEFRONT

There are two fundamental groups of angels: those who are in obedience to God, and those who are in rebellion against Him.

1. How do the angels of God and the angels of Satan contrast? See, for example, Daniel 10:13 and Daniel 12:1. Which group of angels is the more powerful? Why?

_____

_____

_____

_____

2. How do you feel about the warfare imagery used to describe God in the Bible? Read 1 Samuel 17:47; Psalm 24:8; and

Isaiah 13:4. How is the Lord depicted in these verses? Based on what you have learned so far in your study of the spiritual battle between God's elect angels and Satan's fallen angels, what new perspective does this give you about God being a Commander of a great army?

_____

_____

_____

_____

3. Who is ultimately the superior army in this spiritual battle? See Matthew 4:10–11 and Psalm 18:2–3.

_____

_____

_____

4. Read Isaiah 41:10–13 out loud. Then go back and circle phrases in this passage that gave you specific encouragement and comfort in a circumstance you may be facing:

Fear not, for I am with you;
Be not dismayed, for I am your God.
I will strengthen you,
Yes, I will help you,
I will uphold you with My righteous right hand.

Behold, all those who were incensed against you
Shall be ashamed and disgraced;
They shall be as nothing,
And those who strive with you shall perish.

You shall seek them and not find them—
Those who contended with you.
Those who war against you
Shall be as nothing,
As a nonexistent thing.

For I, the LORD your God, will hold your right hand,
Saying to you, "Fear not, I will help you."

ANGELS IN BIBLE PROPHECY

1. Read the following verses and write beside them the angels' announcements:
   - Luke 2:10–11—
   - Luke 24:4–7—
   - Acts 1:11—

2. According to Matthew 24:31, where will the angels be when Christ returns on His Second Coming?

3. What specific future task will be entrusted to the angels, according to Matthew 13:49–50?

THE ANGELS OF REVELATION

Of all the books of the Bible, none illustrate the office, ranks, and assignment of angels more vividly than the book of Revelation.

1. Read Revelation 8:2. How many angels are standing before God in this scene?

_____

_____

2. What were given to these seven angels?

_____

_____

THE TRUMPETS OF JUDGMENT

When the angels blow their trumpets in Revelation, it is not a royal trumpet fanfare. These trumpet blasts sounded the alarm for war. In Numbers 10:9, God instructs the Israelites to announce war with trumpets: "When you go to war in your land against the enemy who oppresses you, then you shall sound an alarm with the trumpets."

The nation of Israel dreaded the trumpets' battle cry. Jeremiah said, "O my soul, my soul! I am pained in my very heart! My heart makes a noise in me; I cannot hold my peace, because you have heard, O my soul, the sound of the trumpet, the alarm of war" (4:19). Joel wrote, "Blow the trumpet in Zion, and sound an alarm in My holy mountain! Let all the inhabitants of the land tremble; for the day of the LORD is coming, for it is at hand" (2:1). The purpose of the angels' trumpets in Revelation is to announce God's judgment against evil.[1]

THE ANGELS AND THE SEVEN TRUMPETS

1. The book of Revelation records that seven angels will blow their trumpets to announce the seven judgments on earth during the Great Tribulation. Read the scriptures below and write out what judgment each angel will announce:
   - First Angel (Revelation 8:7)—
   - Second Angel (Revelation 8:8–9)—
   - Third Angel (Revelation 8:10–11)—
   - Fourth Angel (Revelation 8:12–13)—
   - Fifth Angel (Revelation 9:1–12)—
   - Sixth Angel (Revelation 9:13–18)—
   - Seventh Angel (Revelation 11:15)—

THE ANGELS AND THE SEVEN BOWLS OF JUDGMENTS

1. The book of Revelation also records that seven angels will have seven bowls filled with seven plagues that release the wrath of God. Read the following scriptures and write out what bowl of judgment each angel will pour out on the earth:
   - First Angel (Revelation 16:2)—
   - Second Angel (Revelation 16:3)—
   - Third Angel (Revelation 16:4)—
   - Fourth Angel (Revelation 16:8)—
   - Fifth Angel (Revelation 16:10–11)—
   - Sixth Angel (Revelation 16:12)—
   - Seventh Angel (Revelation 16:17)—

2. Read the following Scripture verses and write out what each angel does as God fulfills His divine plan:
   - Revelation 18:1—

- Revelation 18:21—
- Revelation 19:17–18—
- Revelation 20:1—

3. Finally, what does the angel show to the apostle John in Revelation 21:9–11?

_____

_____

_____

_____

• QUESTIONS FOR GROUP DISCUSSION •

1. Discuss this statement: *The angels of the Lord will protect you at your greatest time of need, no matter your circumstance.* Do you agree or disagree with this statement? Why? Support your answer with biblical references.

2. Have you ever experienced a supernatural intervention that could have been an angel of God protecting you? If so, describe the experience.

3. How did you feel when you read in the book of Revelation about the judgments the angels will announce upon the world? List some of the current world-changing events taking place and how they relate to the biblically prophetic signs of the coming of the Great Tribulation. What could that mean for our generation? Discuss this statement: *The world as we know it is about to come to an end. Everything in God's Word is coming into alignment.*

PRAY

Heavenly Father, we thank You for sending Your angels to protect, defend, and minister to us in our time of need. Give us eyes to see the supernatural power surrounding us as we live out Your divine assignment for our lives. With our voices we declare Your mercy, grace, and loving-kindness. Amen.

ACTION POINTS

1. Think of a difficult circumstance that you or a loved one are experiencing. Now envision the Lord of Hosts on His throne in the Third Heaven, surrounded by multiplied thousands of angels. He is waiting for you to call on Him, and He anticipates you proclaiming His Word over your situation. Don't wait! Call on the Lord today, and He will send His mighty angels to protect and defend you! List the battles you are currently in and present them to the Lord in faith, believing that He will answer.

2. Read 1 Samuel 17:47 out loud. Proclaim the truth of this scripture over your life and the lives of your loved ones today.

3. Look to the heavens and celebrate, child of God! You are not alone! Rejoice and be exceedingly glad, for God's angels are watching over you! In the space below, write out the many times that the Lord has delivered you from your afflictions. Take time to thank Him for His faithfulness.

Week 8
The Third Heaven

STUDY OF CHAPTERS 13–14 IN *THE THREE HEAVENS*

The highest heaven is literally the Third Heaven, which John the Revelator (Revelation 4:1) and the apostle Paul visited.
—John Hagee, *The Three Heavens*

Prepare for Week 8

- Read chapter 13, "The Throne Room of God," in *The Three Heavens*.
- Read chapter 14, "Your Eternal Home," in *The Three Heavens*.

KEY VERSE

I know a man in Christ who fourteen years ago—whether in
the body I do not know, or whether out of the body I do not
know, God knows—such a one was caught up to the third
heaven. And I know such a man—whether in the body
or out of the body I do not know, God knows—how he was
caught up into Paradise and heard inexpressible words,
which it is not lawful for a man to utter.

—2 CORINTHIANS 12:2–4

KEY PASSAGE FROM *THE THREE HEAVENS*

*Christians need to stop thinking of heaven as an invisible place where
the righteous are floating on fluffy white clouds. Instead, we should
imagine the Third Heaven as God sees it. The Architect of the Ages, in
the highest heaven, created a spectacular city with beautiful mansions
of splendor on streets of purest gold since before the beginning of time!*

—*The Three Heavens*, chapter 13

• QUESTIONS FOR PERSONAL STUDY •

CHAPTER 13: THE THRONE ROOM OF GOD

Most people believe in heaven as a place to spend life beyond the grave. It's my opinion that this divine instinct is planted in the human soul by our Creator.

THE NAMES OF HEAVEN

PARADISE

1. Read Luke 23:42–43. By what name did Jesus Christ call the Third Heaven?

_____

_____

2. *Remember: Paradise and the Third Heaven are one and the same place!* How did the apostle Paul describe Paradise in 2 Corinthians 12:4? How did he get there? What did he see and do there?

_____

_____

_____

_____

3. What significant thing is located in Paradise, according to Revelation 2:7?

_____

_____

_____

THE FATHER'S HOUSE

1. Read John 14:2–4. How did Jesus describe His Father's home?

_____

_____

_____

_____

_____

2. Who will be present in "My Father's house" (John 14:2)? What will be prepared for them there?

_____

_____

_____

A HEAVENLY COUNTRY

1. Read Hebrews 11:13–16. What is significant about the contrast between the patriarchs' experiences in their earthly country and the future they looked forward to in "a heavenly country"?

_____

_____

_____

2. Who has prepared this heavenly city? (See Hebrews 11:16.)

_____

_____

THE HEAVENLY CITY

The writer of Hebrews says that God "has prepared a city" for us in the Third Heaven. What does that heavenly city look like?

The apostle John described the New Jerusalem as a city that is foursquare and fourteen hundred miles up, down, and across (Revelation 21:15–18). It would extend from the northernmost point of Maine to the southern tip of Florida, and from the Atlantic Ocean on the east to the western Rocky Mountains. Each street is one-half the length of the diameter of the earth. The levels rise one mile above the others, equaling eight million miles of beautiful golden avenues. The twelve gates of pearl are built upon twelve jeweled foundations (Revelation 21:14), and they will be open to believers from every kindred, tribe, and nation. The tree of life, not seen or enjoyed since Eden, will grow in the center of the city.[1]

WHERE IS THE THIRD HEAVEN?

1. Read 1 Kings 8:23; Luke 2:14; and Ephesians 4:10. From these verses, what did you learn about the direction in which the Third Heaven is located?

2. Read Psalm 75:6. This description of the Third Heaven eliminates three of the four compass points. Which compass point, then, is the Third Heaven?

3. Based on your answer to question #2 above, did you observe anything interesting about the fact that every compass on earth is magnetically attracted to due north?

_____

_____

HEAVEN IS A REAL PLACE

Some say heaven is a state of mind, a dream, or an abstract vision, but Jesus described heaven as a house, a dwelling place (John 14:2). Heaven is not an illusion. It's just as real as the home in which you live right now.

In Acts 1:11, the angel told the disciples, "This same Jesus, who was taken up from you into heaven, will so come in like manner as you saw Him go into heaven." Did Jesus go up in a state of mind? Did He enter an abstraction? No! Jesus went to a real place, an eternal home God has prepared for those who love Him.[2]

THE CHARACTERISTICS OF HEAVEN

1. Read the section "The Characteristics of Heaven" in chapter 13 of *The Three Heavens*. Then write out a short summary beside each characteristic below:

    A Place of Unimaginable Beauty (1 Corinthians 2:9)—

    A Place of Brilliant Light (Revelation 21:23)—

    A Place of Service (Revelation 7:15)—

    A Place of Joy (Psalm 16:11)—

WHAT WILL WE SEE IN HEAVEN?

There are so many beautiful treasures stored up in the Third Heaven awaiting the saints of God (Matthew 6:20)!

1. Read the following scriptures. Beside each one, write the treasure described to be awaiting us in the Third Heaven.
   * John 14:1–3—
   * Hebrews 8:1-2
   * Revelation 5:8–9—
   * Revelation 19:7–10—
   * Revelation 21:2—
   * Revelation 21:21—
   * Revelation 22:1–3—

WHO IS IN THE THIRD HEAVEN?

God the Father is in the Third Heaven sitting on His throne (Revelation 4:2), surrounded by angels singing His praise (7:11). The Third Heaven is His dwelling place.

1. Read Revelation 4:4 and 1 Corinthians 15:42–54. Who else inhabits the Third Heaven with God?

_____

_____

_____

_____

_____

2. Where does Jesus promise that He will also be, in John 14:3? (See also 1 Peter 3:22 and Revelation 3:21.)

_____

_____

_____

THE WONDERS OF THE THIRD HEAVEN

Saint Paul, the brilliant author of thirteen books of the New Testament, was given a guided tour of the celestial city. And when he put his pen to parchment, he still could not describe what God had prepared for those who love Him.

THE WONDER OF WHAT WON'T BE THERE

1. According to Revelation 21:4–5, what is not present in the Third Heaven?

    _____

    _____

    _____

2. What was significant about John's statement in Revelation 21:1, "there was no more sea"? (Take note that the apostle was in exile on the Isle of Patmos, surrounded by the Aegean Sea, when he received God's revelation.)

    _____

    _____

    _____

    _____

THE WONDER OF THE REWARDS

1. In Matthew 5:12, Jesus clearly taught that there will be rewards in heaven. Read the following Scripture passages and write out a short description of each of the following crowns, which will be bestowed by God Himself to His faithful saints:
    *   *Crown of Glory* (1 Peter 5:2–4)—
    *   *Crown of Rejoicing* (Luke 15:10)—

- *Crown of Righteousness* (2 Timothy 4:8)—
- *The Imperishable Crown* (1 Corinthians 9:24–25)—
- *Crown of Life* (James 1:12)—

THE WONDER OF HOW FEW PEOPLE ARE GOING THERE

1. Read Revelation 22:17. How many people are invited to enter into the Third Heaven?

2. What is the warning in Jesus' teaching in Matthew 7:23?

3. Read John 14:6. What is the only way to be assured of a welcomed entrance into the Third Heaven?

THE WONDER OF ETERNAL REST

1. Read Genesis 2:2–3. What did God do on the final day of creation?

2. Read the biblical examples of rest in Exodus 23:12; 1 Kings 5:4; and Matthew 11:28. What did you observe about rest in these verses? List the kinds of rest described.

_____

_____

_____

3. What is one of the purposes of heaven, as described in Revelation 14:13?

_____

_____

_____

4. In contrast to those who are assured of eternal rest, what will happen to those who are not covered by the Blood of the Lamb? (See John 3:36.)

_____

_____

_____

A Place Prepared

Jesus Christ has prepared a place for every born-again believer, and it is located in the Third Heaven.

1. We will all leave this world someday and walk into eternity. The question is, are you ready for heaven? Why or why not?

_____

_____

_____

WEEK 8: THE THIRD HEAVEN

2. What can you do today to be assured that the moment you take your last breath on earth that you will be escorted into the heavenly city prepared for you?

_____

_____

_____

Chapter 14: Your Eternal Home

Death is a rendezvous, a universal appointment. It is the parting of the spirit—from the body and the ultimate path to eternity.

1. Based on your reading of the beginning of chapter 14 in *The Three Heavens*, write a short description of each of the following views toward death:

• Cynicism

_____

• Pessimism

_____

• Morbid preoccupation

_____

• Escapism

_____

2. Do you embrace any of the views listed above? If so, which one(s)? How? Be specific.

_____

_____

_____

_____

3. In the space below, write out your own view about death:

    _____

    _____

    _____

    _____

4. The Bible speaks clearly of the certainty of death and the reality of eternity. In what ways can Christ's death and resurrection affect our personal view of death? (See Romans 6:4–5; Philippians 1:21.)

    _____

    _____

    _____

Two Paths to Eternity

There are two paths that a person can take after death: one is for those who have received Christ as Savior and Lord, and the other is for those who have rejected Him.

1. Look up the word *eternity* in a dictionary and write out the definition below.

    _____

    _____

    _____

2. How do you feel about an existence that goes on forever and ever, with no end? Does the thought of eternity make you

feel excited, hopeful, or joyful or anxious, worried, or fearful? Describe your feelings below.

_____

_____

_____

_____

3. Write out your personal response to the following question: *We will all die, and we will all enter our eternal home; the issue is,* which one?

_____

_____

_____

_____

THE PLACE CALLED HELL

Hell is a real place; in fact, I know many people who spend much of their time telling other people how to get there!

1. Read Luke 16:19–26. What did you learn about Hades (another name for hell) in this passage? Where is hell located? What is it like there? How do the residents of hell feel? Write out below how Jesus describes the place called hell.

_____

_____

_____

_____

2. According to Proverbs 11:7, what happens when a wicked person dies? What dies along with them?

_____
_____
_____
_____

THE LAKE OF FIRE
Hell and the Lake of Fire are two different places.

1. Read Matthew 25:41; Revelation 19:20; and Revelation 20:10, 14–15. How is the Lake of Fire described in these verses? What did you observe from these passages about God's purpose for the Lake of Fire?

_____
_____
_____

2. Read Revelation 20:11–15. What did you learn from this passage about the Great White Throne Judgment (for unbelievers)?

_____
_____
_____

3. Remember, Christians will not participate in the Great White Throne Judgment. Believers' judgment takes place before Christ's Millennial Kingdom. Read 2 Corinthians

5:10 and write out what you learn about the Judgment Seat of Christ.

_____

_____

_____

_____

4. Will a Christian be condemned in the Judgment Seat of Christ? Why or why not? Read John 5:24 and Romans 8:1 to support your answer.

_____

_____

_____

FOUR BLOOD MOONS

In my book Four Blood Moons: Something Is About to Change, *I describe in great detail the supernatural connection of celestial events to biblical prophecy—the future of God's chosen people and that of the nations of the world.*

1. Three Tetrads (a series of four consecutive Blood Moons) have appeared in the past five hundred years that have coincided with the Jewish Feasts. The years are recorded below. Beside each year, write the historical event that relates to the Jewish people.
   - 1492—
   - 1948—
   - 1967—

2. We have experienced the fourth and final Tetrad in the twenty-first century that was linked to the Feasts of the Lord. What are a few of the historically significant events that occurred during the 2014–2015 appearances of the Four Blood Moons? How do these events relate to the Jewish people?

_____

_____

_____

3. Read Joel 2:31 and Luke 21:25–38. What did you observe from these passages about the significance of "blood moons" to the coming day of the Lord ?

_____

_____

WE SHALL SEE HIM

When the redeemed get to heaven, "we shall see Him as He is"—as the Lord of glory, high and lifted up, full of grace and truth. As the Alpha and the Omega, the First and the Last! We shall see Him as the Lamb of God, the Light of the world, the Lord of glory, the Lion of Judah!

1. Read 1 John 3:2. What is the difference between seeing Jesus during His earthly ministry and seeing Jesus "as He is"?

_____

_____

_____

2. Are you ready to stand before God in the judgment as a son or daughter of the Father's royal family? If so, rejoice! Your eternal destiny is secure in the Third Heaven with Almighty God! If not, make the decision today, and listen as the angels in heaven rejoice!

• QUESTIONS FOR GROUP DISCUSSION •

1. Discuss the following: *We will all leave this world one day and walk into eternity; what then? Will you open your eyes in the majesty of the Third Heaven and be with your heavenly Father, or will you be lost forever in outer darkness without God?* What are your answers to these important questions?

2. If you are not certain that you will spend eternity in Heaven at the moment of your death then go to the end of chapter 14 of *The Three Heavens* book and repeat the prayer of salvation.

3. What insights did you gain about God's character as you studied the Third Heaven? What specific things stood out to you?

PRAY

Heavenly Father, may we know with absolute confidence that Your Son is the way, the truth, and the life and that no one comes to the Father but through Him. Jesus is the Prince of Peace and the hope of glory. He is the good news and the source of our joy—the King of kings and Lord of lords. May we go forth and walk in the assurance that when we take our final breath on earth, we will see You in all Your glory and spend eternity with Jesus Christ, our Savior, in the Third Heaven. Amen.

ACTION POINTS

1. In this study you have learned that God created Three Heavens, each one higher than the other: the First Heaven that we can see with our eyes; the Second Heaven, where Satan and his demons are temporarily working against God's saints; and the Third Heaven, where God dwells. You have learned how to take action with the knowledge you have gained from this study. Now write down what you believe God expects you to accomplish with this newfound understanding.

2. Go back through the "Action Points" suggestions in weeks 1–7 and review them. Is there something you haven't yet done? Make a plan to do it now! Don't let this opportunity pass you by.

PART TWO

EXPLORING THE SIGNIFICANCE
OF THE THREE HEAVENS IN
THE LIFE OF A BELIEVER

9

The Word of God and the Three Heavens

By faith we understand that the worlds were framed
by the word of God, so that the things which are seen
were not made of things which are visible.

HEBREWS 11:3

We have clearly established the reality of the Three Heavens—
each one higher than the other. In this brief chapter, I provide
further scriptural support substantiating the existence of the
Three Heavens to supplement and enhance your personal study.

THE FIRST HEAVEN

*God said, "Let there be lights in the firmament of the heavens to
divide the day from the night; and let them be for signs and seasons,
and for days and years; and let them be for lights in the firmament of
the heavens to give light on the earth"; and it was so. Then God made
two great lights: the greater light to rule the day, and the lesser light to
rule the night. He made the stars also.*

—Genesis 1:14–16

I have made the earth,
And created man on it.
I—My hands—stretched out the heavens,
And all their host I have commanded.

—Isaiah 45:12

Thus says the LORD,
Who gives the sun for a light by day,
The ordinances of the moon and the stars for a light by night,
Who disturbs the sea,
And its waves roar
(The LORD of hosts is His name).

—Jeremiah 31:35

When I consider Your heavens, the work of Your fingers,
The moon and the stars, which You have ordained,
What is man that You are mindful of him,
And the son of man that You visit him?
For You have made him a little lower than the angels,
And You have crowned him with glory and honor.

You have made him to have dominion over the works of Your hands;
You have put all things under his feet.

—Psalm 8:3–6

He has set a tabernacle for the sun. . . .
Its rising is from one end of heaven,
And its circuit to the other end;
And there is nothing hidden from its heat.

—Psalm 19:4, 6

Out of the ground the LORD God formed every beast of the field and
every bird of the air, and brought them to Adam to see what he would
call them. And whatever Adam called each living creature, that was
its name.

—Genesis 2:19

He has appointed the moon for seasons.

—Psalm 104:19

You shall take with you seven each of every clean animal, a male and his female; two each of animals that are unclean, a male and his female; also seven each of birds of the air, male and female, to keep the species alive on the face of all the earth.

—Genesis 7:2–3

You have made him to have dominion over the works of Your hands;
You have put all things under his feet,
All sheep and oxen—
Even the beasts of the field,
The birds of the air,
And the fish of the sea
That pass through the paths of the seas.

—Psalm 8:6–8

THE SECOND HEAVEN

Says He who has the sharp two-edged sword: "I know your works, and where you dwell, where Satan's throne is."

—Revelation 2:12–13

And I looked, and I heard an angel flying through the midst of heaven, saying with a loud voice, "Woe, woe, woe to the inhabitants of the earth, because of the remaining blasts of the trumpet of the three angels who are about to sound!"

—Revelation 8:13

Then [the angel] said to me, "Do not fear, Daniel, for from the first day that you set your heart to understand, and to humble yourself before your God, your words were heard; and I have come because of your words. But the prince of the kingdom of Persia withstood me twenty-one days; and behold, Michael, one of the chief princes, came to help me, for I had been left alone there with the kings of Persia."

—Daniel 10:12–13

Now when the Pharisees heard it they said, "This fellow does not cast out demons except by Beelzebub, the ruler of the demons."

But Jesus knew their thoughts, and said to them: "Every kingdom divided against itself is brought to desolation, and every city or house divided against itself will not stand. If Satan casts out Satan, he is divided against himself. How then will his kingdom stand?"

—Matthew 12:24–26

THE THIRD HEAVEN

Indeed heaven and the highest heavens belong to the LORD your God, also the earth with all that is in it.

—Deuteronomy 10:14

For you have said in your heart:
"I will ascend into heaven,
I will exalt my throne above the stars of God;
I will also sit on the mount of the congregation
On the farthest sides of the north."

—Isaiah 14:13

Look down from Your holy habitation, from heaven, and bless Your
people Israel and the land which You have given us.

—Deuteronomy 26:15

LORD God of Israel, there is no God in heaven above or on earth
below like You, who keep Your covenant and mercy with Your ser-
vants who walk before You with all their hearts.

—1 Kings 8:23

You alone are the LORD;
You have made heaven,
The heaven of heavens, with all their host,
The earth and everything on it,
The seas and all that is in them,
And You preserve them all.
The host of heaven worships You.

—Nehemiah 9:6

Is not God in the height of heaven?

—Job 22:12

In My Father's house are many mansions; if it were not so, I would
have told you. I go to prepare a place for you. And if I go and pre-
pare a place for you, I will come again and receive you to Myself;
that where I am, there you may be also.

—John 14:2–3

Jesus said to him, "Assuredly, I say to you, today you will be with
Me in Paradise."

—Luke 23:43

I know a man in Christ who fourteen years ago—whether in the body I do not know, or whether out of the body I do not know, God knows—such a one was caught up to the third heaven. And I know such a man—whether in the body or out of the body I do not know, God knows— how he was caught up into Paradise and heard inexpressible words, which it is not lawful for a man to utter.

—2 Corinthians 12:2–4

But will God indeed dwell on the earth? Behold, heaven and the heaven of heavens cannot contain You. How much less this temple which I have built!

—1 Kings 8:27

He who descended is also the One who ascended far above all the heavens, that He might fill all things.

—Ephesians 4:10

These all died in faith, not having received the promises, but having seen them afar off were assured of them, embraced them and confessed that they were strangers and pilgrims on the earth. For those who say such things declare plainly that they seek a homeland. And truly if they had called to mind that country from which they had come out, they would have had opportunity to return. But now they desire a better, that is, a heavenly country. Therefore God is not ashamed to be called their God, for He has prepared a city for them.

—Hebrews 11:13–16

To him who overcomes I will give to eat from the tree of life, which is in the midst of the Paradise of God.

—Revelation 2:7

10

Identifying Demons

Too many modern Christians have no concept of why Jesus Christ came to this earth. Too long have we portrayed Him as gentle Jesus, meek and mild, with lily-white hands too pure to become stained with the social or spiritual controversy of His day or ours.

The Jesus Christ of the New Testament thundered into His public ministry without public acceptance. Imagine the gall of some fanatic with a whip in His hand breaking up the church bingo game, shouting in anger, "'My house shall be called a house of prayer,' but you have made it a 'den of thieves'" (Matthew 21:13). Consider the noble Son of God as He stooped in the sand to aid a prostitute while pious preachers hovered like buzzards around a carcass, with rocks in hand prepared to do what they considered to be the will of God. Jesus came with teachings and parables that shattered society's norms, and many are still fractured and out of tune with the divine symphony our Lord has orchestrated.

The fact is that the institutional church today is completely in discord with the Jesus of the New Testament. He advanced mind-staggering declarations like: we grow by giving (Matthew 6:4; Luke 6:38); we gain by losing (Matthew 16:25); we go up by going down (Matthew 23:12); and we live by dying (Matthew 10:39; John 12:25). For two thousand years we have been reading what He said without fully understanding it, much less believing or doing it.

Jesus Christ spent much of His time casting out demons and

189

delivering people from the bondage of evil spirits. He dealt with demonized persons often, publicly, and successfully. However, the institutional church ignores this reality and many self-righteous Christians are repulsed at the very thought of their susceptibility to demonic influences. The time has come for the church to choose between its dignity or God's deliverance.

SCRIPTURAL EVIDENCE OF DEMONS AND DELIVERANCE

I challenge every serious student of the Bible to examine the Scripture and record the number of times Jesus Christ delivered people from demons or evil spirits. In the writings of Luke, Jesus came from the wilderness "in the power of the Spirit" (Luke 4:14) and immediately went to Capernaum and cast out evil spirits from a man who was in the worship service (Luke 4:33–36). As soon as Jesus left the synagogue He went to Simon Peter's home, ate supper, and again cast out demon spirits (Luke 4:38–41). Twice in one day He delivered people who were bound by demons.

That was not a rare occasion. Examine for yourself how often Christ performed the ministry of deliverance or enabled others to do so with complete success. Compare the following scriptures with the understanding that "evil spirits" or "devils" mean the same as demons. To bring home this fact, highlight in your Bible the various times Jesus successfully dealt with demons:

In the Gospel of Matthew:
    4:24; 7:22; 8:16, 28–33; 9:32–34; 10:8; 11:18; 12:22, 24, 27–28; 15:22, 28; 17:18

In the Gospel of Mark:
1:32, 34, 39; 3:15, 22; 5:12, 15–16, 18; 6:13; 7:26, 29–30; 9:38; 16:9, 17

In the Gospel of Luke:
4:33–35, 41; 7:33; 8:2, 27–38; 9:1, 42, 49; 10:17; 11:14–15, 18-20; 13:32

In the Gospel of John:
7:20; 8:48–49, 52; 10:20–21

In the letters of Paul:
1 Corinthians 10:20–21:1; Timothy 4:1

In the book of James:
2:19; 3:15

In the book of Revelation:
9:20; 16:14; 18:2

Without a doubt the Scripture declares that demons are real and their expulsion is possible! If all Scripture is profitable (2 Timothy 3:16) and Christ is our perfect example, why did the Holy Spirit move upon the authors of this sacred manuscript to allow such enormous coverage of this special ministry? The apostle Paul gives the answer, "That the man of God may be complete, thoroughly equipped for every good work" (2 Timothy 3:17). These scriptures are the sounding of an alarm that demons were active in the ministry of Jesus Christ and are still active in the world today.

PROPHETIC EVIDENCE OF DEMONS

Jesus established that He would not only cast out demons during His ministry on earth but would also give the believer the ability to do so through the power of His name until His triumphant return. Jesus said to the Pharisees, "Behold, I cast out demons and perform cures today and tomorrow, and the third *day* I shall be perfected" (Luke 13:32). The time measurement of a "day" used here is explained further by the apostle Peter, who reflected on the length of God's day by stating, "Beloved, do not forget this one thing, that with the Lord one day is as a thousand years, and a thousand years as one day" (2 Peter 3:8). Therefore, the length of a day could be interpreted as a thousand years.

With that in mind, what was Jesus declaring in Luke 13:32? That if, "I cast out demons . . . today and tomorrow [or for the next two thousand years], and on the third day [the millennial reign] I shall be perfected," the church in the twenty-first century would still find it necessary to cast out demons! And could it be that the established church has erred, not knowing what Scripture says about the ongoing influence of demons (Mark 12:24) and our authority over them?

Further scriptural evidence of the existence of demons in our time is found in 2 Timothy 3:1–9. The apostle Paul begins in verse 1 by declaring that he is about to describe conditions that will exist in the "last days": "But know this, that in the last days perilous times will come." During the next six verses Paul vividly describes the conditions of this present age as accurately as could any contemporary author. In verse eight, Paul speaks of Jannes and Jambres, who contended with Moses, as "types" or "shadows" of personalities that would be around tormenting the church in the last days. Who were Jannes and Jambres? They were magicians of Pharaoh who contested Moses and exercised satanic power until God stopped them (Exodus 7:11–12; 8:7, 18–19). This is another scriptural confirmation that the church will battle demonic powers and personalities in the last days.

From this Bible evidence, we can draw several conclusions. One, the Devil is alive and well, and his legions of demons are very real and active today. Second, Jesus Christ dealt with demons everywhere He went (Mark 1:39). And third, Jesus cast out demons publicly, having complete power and authority over them. It was a normal part of His ministry (Matthew 4:22–25; 28:18; 10:1).

GREATER WORKS

Did Christ intend for the deliverance of demons to stop at the Cross? Absolutely not! Listen to the voice of the Master:

> *Most assuredly, I say to you, he who believes in Me, the works that I do he will do also; and greater works than these he will do, because I go to My Father. (John 14:12)*

Christ further exhorts the believer with this command: "And these signs will follow those who believe: In My name they will cast out demons" (Mark 16:17). Are you a believer? If so, you're in spiritual combat with demon personalities! The apostles and the New Testament church had complete authority and power over demon spirits. Christ said every believer has that power and authority and they will do "greater works" than He did. Therefore, if Christ hasn't changed His mind about believers expelling demons, and Satan hasn't changed his purpose to destroy the church, then who has changed?

The finger of judgment points squarely in the face of our lukewarm, modern-day church, which is described in Scripture as "having a form of godliness but denying its power" (2 Timothy 3:5). We, through our unwillingness to confront demons, have signed a truce with Satan when what is actually required is a declaration of war.

THE AUTHORITY OF THE BELIEVER

But God, being rich in mercy, because of His great love with which He loved us, even when we were dead in our transgressions, made us alive together with Christ (by grace you have been saved), and raised us up with Him, and seated us with Him in the heavenly places Christ Jesus, so that in the ages to come He might show the surpassing riches of His grace in kindness toward us in Christ Jesus. (Ephesians 2:4–7 NASB)

Believers have long underestimated our authority in spiritual warfare. Authority over the power of darkness is the possession of every child of God. A believer who is fully aware of the *Power* that stands behind him or her can face the Enemy without fear or uncertainty.

We are living in desperate times, but we don't need to take desperate measures to be victorious—for the Lord declares that the battle belongs to Him (2 Chronicles 20:15)! At the Cross

Jesus declared victory when He conquered death, hell, and the grave—and that undeniable victory He shares with us!

The Cross revealed three very important truths: the ultimate obedience of Christ to His Father, the atonement for our sin, and the crushing defeat of the enemies of divine authority. Christ sits at the right hand of God and every believer therefore occupies "with Him" the same eminent position (Ephesians 2:4–6 NASB).

Remember this truth: we share in Christ the authority that He has over the powers of darkness. It is time that we stand in this divinely appointed position and apply it over our lives and the lives of our loved ones!

An illustration comes to mind that I heard many years ago as a young boy in a rural church in Channelview, Texas. A certain building contractor had done an extensive amount of work for a local church and was having great difficulty collecting his fee. After several fruitless attempts to get his money he decided to take extreme action. He rented a red Devil costume and went to the indebted church after the Sunday evening service was well under way. Entering the rear of the building in his Devil costume, he made his way to the electrical panels that controlled the lighting. At a precise moment, he switched off all the lights and sprang onto the platform roaring like a lion. The bright moonlight caused his red suit to glow devilishly.

People ran in terror. The congregation stampeded for the door without dignity or reservation, with the pastor leading the way.

One elderly lady too feeble to compete with the stampede

knelt at the feet of the contractor-turned-Devil. "Oh, Mr. Devil," she said, "I've worked in this church faithfully for years. I've taught the junior boys' Sunday school class, baked pies for every bake sale, and even cut the church grass when I was younger. But in spite of all that, Mr. Devil, I want you to know from the bottom of my heart I was on your side all the time."

This precious woman chose to take sides with the enemy rather than fight, for fear she was too tired for the battle and too weak to win. The Bride of Christ is neither! We are to be ready for the fight—we must run and not grow weary! We are to enter the battle believing that the victory is ours! It is time for the church to choose—dignity or deliverance, the ritual of the church or the reality of His Word.

It is time to recognize the invasion of demons in our society and then take our rightful authority over them!

THE ANATOMY OF AN ADVERSARY

Demons are quick to recognize believers who are armed with the authority of the Lord to expose and defeat them. And, in like manner, every believer should be able to recognize the evil spirits that dwell among us.

What does a demon look like? Does a demon have a personality and self-awareness? If so, what are the limits of his intelligence and power over men? The war will be won or lost on our knowledge of the enemy.

Christians, you are at war! We must examine the anatomy of our adversaries.

Demons Have Personality
(See Luke 4:34.)

Emotion, will, knowledge, self-realization, and patterns of reaction are a few of the components of a personality. The Scripture shows us that demons have personalities.

Demons possess supernatural knowledge. When Jesus entered the synagogue in Capernaum on the Sabbath, a demonized person was present and made this statement: "What have we to do with You, Jesus of Nazareth? Did You come to destroy us? I know who You are—the Holy One of God!" (Luke 4:34). No one else present knew who Jesus was since it was His first trip to Capernaum. No one there knew He was the Son of God except the demon in the man. Even the disciples were not sure who Jesus was but the demon announced to everyone that they were in the presence of the Holy One of God.

A demonized man at Ephesus demonstrated great knowledge when he said to the seven sons of Sceva, "Jesus I know, and Paul I know; but who are you?" (Acts 19:15). The sons of Sceva were Jewish exorcists who were trying to cast out demons in the name of Jesus, whom Paul preached. But these men only aroused the demons in this man, causing him to tear their clothes off, beat them, and send them running for their lives into the street naked.

This kind of spiritism does not come from a human source—it comes from Satan. We are warned in the Scripture to stay completely away from persons who practice divination (Deuteronomy 18:10–11). God uses His Word to provide us with the knowledge of the future that He wants us to have, any other source is satanic and demonic (Leviticus 20:6 NASB).

DEMONS HAVE A WILL
(SEE "WHAT CHARACTERIZES DEMONS?" CHAPTER 5 IN
THE THREE HEAVENS.)

Jesus said that when demons are outside of the human body they walk through dry places seeking rest. When the demon can't find rest, he decides, "I will return to my house from which I came" (Matthew 12:44). The demon recognized that the human body was his house, and it was his will to return to the house. When the demoniac of Gadara approached Jesus, the demons seized the vocal cords of the man and begged Jesus not to send them to hell (Luke 8:31) but to allow them to enter other host bodies, which, in this case, were swine (v. 33). This is an example of demons exercising self-determination and will. They did not want to go to hell; they wanted to go into the swine. While teaching this subject, I once told my congregation that this was the greatest serving of deviled ham in the history of mankind.

A demon's will is expressed through the body he controls. If a demon desires to murder, then he must have a body to murder through. If the demon of lust wills to commit adultery, then he does so through the human agency he controls.

A young girl in India brazenly insisted that she wanted to dance for a group of missionaries. She threw her head wrap to the ground in preparation for the dance. Detecting a demonic presence, a Christian worker commanded the evil spirit to leave her in the name of Jesus Christ. The girl fell immediately to the ground. After a few minutes she sat up, pulling the head wrap over her face very modestly. The missionary helped her to her feet and asked, "Why were you lying on the ground?"

"I don't know," she replied.

"Will you dance for me?" the missionary asked, testing her.

"No," she replied. "I do not know how to dance."[1] She had been dancing through the will of the demon within her that was now cast out.

When I was in seminary, a great tragedy occurred in the life of one of the members of a local church in Houston, Texas. A young girl who had been raised in the church all of her life and who never displayed any abnormal behavior, came home from school one day and, without giving a word of warning or reason, shot her mother to death with a twelve-gauge shotgun. When asked by police why she had done so when there were no arguments, no disagreements, nor a single exchange of words, she simply said, "A voice told me to get the gun and shoot my mother!"

It is important to realize that church membership does not protect a person from demonic influence. A demon can exercise his will in the life of any person who opens the door.

DEMONS HAVE EMOTION
(SEE "WHAT CHARACTERIZES DEMONS?" CHAPTER 5 IN THE THREE HEAVENS.)

When the demons in the body of the Gadarene man came into the presence of Jesus Christ, they were terrified. The Bible says, "When he saw Jesus, he cried out, fell down before Him, and with a loud voice said, 'What have I to do with You, Jesus, Son of the Most High God? I beg You, do not torment me!'" (Luke 8:28). Demons are terrified of the power of Jesus Christ, and the mere mention of His name causes them to tremble. The apostle James wrote, "Even the demons believe—and tremble!" (James 2:19).

Derek Prince, an authority on demonology, once shared this story. A demonized woman who had never been to East Africa told Derek things that would have been impossible for anyone to know unless they had been in that country. When he began to cast the evil spirit from her, she started hopping away from him just like an East African bird, saying, "Don't touch me, don't touch me!" The demon displayed an emotional outburst due to the fear of losing its host.

DEMONS HAVE THE ABILITY TO SPEAK
(SEE "WHAT CHARACTERIZES DEMONS?" CHAPTER 5 IN
THE THREE HEAVENS.)

Demons have the power to control the vocal cords of their subjects and speak through them (Mark 1:24; Acts 19:15). Demons can speak in a foreign tongue and understand the same. It is not uncommon for a woman's voice to be very deep when taken over by demonic forces, and a man's voice to be very different from his normal speaking voice.

A Bolivian missionary was invited by a man with whom he had prayed many times to join a "prayer gathering" in his home. However, the missionary recognized that the prayer meeting was actually a séance when a demon spoke through his host in a different voice and said, "Good evening! We are very glad to have the minister with us. He has done many kindnesses to this body [the missionary had prayed for the man several times before], and we are grateful for it!"

This began a lengthy battle between the missionary and the demons within the man. Whenever the missionary cast out one demon, another spirit would come forward from the same man with a completely different sounding voice. Eventually, the missionary cast out all the demons inhabiting his friend.[2]

DEMONS HAVE NAMES AND SELF-AWARENESS (SEE "WHAT CHARACTERIZES DEMONS?" CHAPTER 5 IN *THE THREE HEAVENS*.)

When Jesus was confronted by the demons within the Gadarene, the Lord asked for a name. "He asked him, "What is your name?" And he [the demon] answered, saying, "My name is Legion; for we are many" (Mark 5:9). It is not uncommon for demon spirits to surrender their names to ministers and missionaries upon demand. Several missionary friends have shared with me that demons actually name themselves as they leave the body.

All demons have definite depraved passions and have given their names and characteristics with such regularity that they have been classified into groups. These groups of demons can be divided into the following:

DECEIT: Lying, deception, pretense, exaggeration, falsehood, hypocrisy, craftiness, fakery, trickery.

FEARS: Fear of people, darkness, being alone, suffering, the future, the unknown, dying, claustrophobia, bondage, and constraint. Some of the ways demons express themselves are through doubt, unbelief, trembling, restlessness, and an overwhelming feeling of torment.

MALICE AND HATRED: Strife, anger, envy, mischievousness, jealousy, disputing, backbiting, contempt, temper tantrums, resentment, despising, derision, stubbornness, opposition, division, impudence, rebelliousness, spite.

PRIDE: Haughtiness, vanity, defiance, scorn, arrogance, boastfulness, covetousness, vainglory, conceit, indignation, mockery.

SELF: Self-consciousness, self-conceit, self-pity, selfishness, self-righteousness, self-sufficiency, self-justification, self-content, inferiority, bitterness, slackness, false security, false peace, murmuring, shame, neglect.

PSYCHOLOGICAL: Double-mindedness, derangement, mental weakness, vain imaginations, confusion, hypnosis, seared conscience, temper, misunderstanding, inferiority, schizophrenia, depression, uncanny laughter.

DRUGS: Cravings and addictions to drugs.

DRINK: Excessive craving for and addiction to alcohol.

SPIRITUALISTIC: Fortune-telling, Ouija board, psychic reading, witchcraft, spiritualism, medium, palm reading, voodoo, enchantment, tea leaves, crystal ball.

GAMBLING: The obsession with wagering.

VIOLENCE: Vengeance, strife, murder, suicide, death, abusive behavior.

SEXUAL: Lust, sexual indulgence, filthiness, passion, abuse, impurity, fornication, lasciviousness, carnality, defilement, vulgarity, filthy conversation, filthy thoughts, sodomy.

HERESY: The worship of various cults and religions, false doctrine, religious statues, idolatry, apostasy, persecution, religious delusion, misinterpretation, willful disobedience.

THEFT: Robbery, pickpocketing, shoplifting, scamming.[3]

I have listed several groups and characteristics of demonic activity but certainly not all of them. My purpose is to make you aware of the various ways you are susceptible to evil spirits.

DEMONS HAVE PHYSICAL POWER
(SEE ACTS 19:16.)

Demonized people have supernatural physical strength. The man who burst into our church with the loaded gun, intending to commit murder (described in "The Shooter" in chapter 7 of *The Three Heavens*) possessed superhuman physical power. He was violently tackled to the ground by a muscular church member and restrained by several other men but wasn't even slightly shaken.

I personally experienced the physical power of demons when I was called to minister to a demonized woman in our city. When I arrived, she was silent and staring into space as if in a daze. At regular intervals she would scream with such violence my flesh rippled with goose bumps. I walked over to the chair where she was sitting, and she reached out and grasped my arm.

She was a petite woman, and I weigh well over two hundred pounds, yet she almost jerked me off my feet. This power is not imagined. It's real and very supernatural.

This fact of power is evidenced in Luke's gospel. Describing the demon-possessed man in Gadara, Luke observes, "He had often been bound with shackles and chains. And the chains had been pulled apart by him, and the shackles broken in pieces; neither could anyone tame him" (Mark 5:4).

A seventeen-year-old boy in the village of Tabasco, Mexico, suffered attacks that would come about dusk and last until midnight. During the attacks he would see various kinds of animals coming toward him and would lose his personality as demon powers possessed him. These attacks began with severe pain in his abdomen for which there was no natural explanation. One evening, sitting on the edge of his bed, he looked at his close friends and asked, "Who are you? I'm stronger than all of you!" It took eight men to hold him to the bed. After they were completely exhausted, another shift of men came to hold down the teenage boy. After four hours of continuous wrestling, seventeen grown men were exhausted, but the young boy was fresh and strong.[4]

Does Satan have that much supernatural power? God's Word plainly states that in the last days Satan will deceive multitudes by performing signs and wonders. He will allow his servants to call down fire from heaven (Revelation 13:13) and to give life to a statue, causing it to speak (Revelation 13:15). John the Revelator's blunt declaration, "They are spirits of demons, performing signs" (Revelation 16:14), confirms that they have phenomenal power for the world to witness.

DEMONS ARE SPIRITS
(SEE LUKE 24:39.)

Jesus said to Thomas in the Upper Room, "A spirit does not have flesh and bones as you see I have" (Luke 24:39). Demons are a part of Satan's spiritual Kingdom and as such have no material body. They are identified many times in Scripture as spirits. The apostle Paul projects the profile of our powerful enemy with these words: "For we do not wrestle against flesh and blood, but against . . . spiritual hosts of wickedness in the heavenly places" (Ephesians 6:12). Demons are the "spiritual hosts of wickedness" who perform Satan's will on earth.

11
Expelling Demons

In the fall of 1963, Joseph "Joe Cargo" Valachi testified before a Senate subcommittee and publicly acknowledged for the first time ever the existence of the Mafia and its activities in the United States. Law enforcement officials were stunned by the makeup and muscle of this well-defined covert organization. Finally this hidden society had been exposed to the world.

Valachi gave a descriptive account detailing how the Mafia was controlled by "families" who gave orders to "enforcers," who then marshaled "street soldiers" to accomplish any type of criminal crusade desired. The Mafia had infiltrated big business with money acquired through drug trafficking, gambling, and prostitution. Their influence and financial power controlled many prominent citizens and penetrated every level of government from the office of dogcatcher to the judge's chambers.

The point is this—the Mafia had been operating in the United States for decades with unlimited force and influence and no one knew! The identity of those running the organization was a complete mystery even to the Attorney General of the United States and the FBI.

However, before the Mafia could be fought, they had to be exposed and recognized. Satan and his demons are much like the Mafia in that they have evil intent, they are highly organized, and they have enormous power. Valachi blew the whistle on the Mafia and gave accurate details, and the apostle Paul exposed Satan and his demons with piercing accuracy.

RECOGNIZING THE ENEMY

Before you can resist demons, you must be able to recognize them.

The day following the shooting incident in my church (told in "The Shooter," chapter 7 of *The Three Heavens*), the bold headlines in our local newspaper screamed, "Demon Sermon Halted!" With the additional assistance of radio and television, the general public in our city became very curious about demonic activity in this country. The prevailing question people were asking me at the time was: "How do you recognize demonic activity?" Nothing has changed.

There are certain rules that will help a person recognize the presence of demons. The first is that *demonized people are driven and mastered by a power beyond their control.* Demon-possessed people are helpless to control themselves. For example, when a woman is possessed with a perverse demon she may regret every immoral sexual act yet will continuously repeat them because the demon power within has absolutely enslaved her. A man who is possessed with a demon of anger may apologize with tears brimming in his eyes, yet repeatedly he reaches a point where he is completely driven to curse at his loved ones, smash his fist through the wall, kick the door off its hinges, and break every dish within his reach. He will over and over again regret his behavior and ask for forgiveness, yet the monster within masters him with ruthless dictatorship and will strike over and over again!

Another rule is that *demonized people are very restless and resentful in the presence of prayer, Bible reading, or spiritual conversation.* Demonized people have been known on many occasions to tear a Bible to shreds, chop a cross to splinters, and violently curse a praying minister. The demon within who masters them is at war with the power of God—thus the clash of the two Kingdoms.

A third rule is that *demonized people rarely profess, "There's a demon within me!"* It's very important to understand this point because far too many people tend to blame every adverse situation on the Devil and his demons. This attitude does not lend itself to spiritual balance. Additionally, be very careful of novice Christians who volunteer that certain persons or situations are demonic. Spiritual discernment is essential during such encounters.

A demon does not want to be detected since it craves to inhabit the human body and master the human will. It will not purposely draw attention to itself; demons are much more subtle than that. However, when a tormented person reaches out to a Christian who is equipped with the knowledge and discernment offered in the Scriptures to recognize and deal with demonic activity, then the demon upon command in the name of Jesus will reveal its name.

DELIVERANCE FROM THE ENEMY

"Is there any hope for deliverance, Pastor Hagee?" The tortured voice was desperately searching for some relief to his monstrous behavior. I was overjoyed to tell him that there was glorious relief in the victorious Christ.

If the knowledge found in this book has confirmed your suspicions of supernatural powers trying to invade your life or the life of a loved one, then I have wonderful news: "Whosoever shall call on the name of the LORD shall be delivered" (Joel 2:32 KJV).

Here are some essential truths that will set the captive free.

KNOW WHAT TO DO

First, allow the Holy Spirit to guide you. It is essential to make a proper assessment. Not every situation is controlled by demonic activity. There are some outward similarities between people who have physical or emotional conditions to those who are under demonic influence. In order to properly identify the enemy, submission to your delegated spiritual authority and personal prayer and fasting are all key factors in determining the best course of action.

GOD'S POWER IS ESSENTIAL

Jesus confessed, "If I cast out demons by the Spirit of God, surely the kingdom of God has come upon you" (Matthew 12:28). The Master Himself recognized that it requires spiritual power to expel demons. The emphatic necessity of spiritual power is proven in Luke's fourth chapter. He writes that "Jesus, being filled with the Holy Spirit" went into the wilderness to face the insidious temptations of Satan himself (v. 1). Jesus overcame Satan by spiritual power and scriptural truth.

"Then Jesus returned in the power of the Spirit" (Luke 4:14) and went to His hometown to begin His public ministry. When He stood and addressed the membership of His synagogue, He said, "The Spirit of the Lord is upon me . . . to preach deliverance to the captives" (4:18 KJV). Jesus Christ, who knew all things and was incapable of making a wrong decision, testified that Satan must be met in the power of the Holy Spirit.

The Power of the Name of Jesus

Christ has given every Spirit-led believer a blank check and challenges him to fill in his request. "Whatever you ask the Father in My name He will give you" (John 16:23).

We are to cast out demons in the authority of Jesus' name. "In My name they will cast out demons" (Mark 16:17). When Jesus sent out the seventy believers to minister, the seventy returned to Jesus and said, "Lord, even the demons are subject to us in Your name" (Luke 10:17). When Paul was confronted with a demonized woman at Philippi, he used the authority of Jesus' name to expel the spirit from the woman: "I command you in the name of Jesus Christ to come out of her" (Acts 16:18).

It is important to note that Jesus only placed His hands upon the physically ill, but those possessed by evil spirits He addressed by word of command. Likewise, believers should not make physical contact with a person under demonic influence.

Three Primary Actions to Freedom

Freedom from the demonic strongholds of Satan first requires action from the person in spiritual bondage. The Bible clearly states the steps that must be followed.

Confession Is a Must!

The scriptural sequence is that confession goes before prayer. The person who is asking for deliverance must first make a full and honest confession of his sin before God. "If we confess our sins, He is faithful and just to forgive us our sins and to cleanse us from all unrighteousness" (1 John 1:9). Solomon declares, "He who covers his sins will not prosper, but whoever confesses and forsakes them will have mercy" (Proverbs 28:13).

If the demonized person refuses to confess his wrongdoing or states he doesn't need God then there is no reason to go on. Our Father in heaven is the only source of hope—to refuse His forgiveness and grace is to accept demonic dictatorship.

Additionally, if a person has been involved in the practice of occult rituals, I often lead them in a prayer of denunciation. This prayer amounts to a formal spiritual divorce from Satan and his Kingdom. Be forewarned the demon may react violently as it resists expulsion. There may be unexplained coughing or even vomiting. Most demons do not exit peacefully.

FORGIVENESS IS A MUST!

The next requirement is to completely forgive. Before you can receive forgiveness, you must be willing to extend forgiveness to others. The Lord's Prayer reveals the secret of true forgiveness with these words: "Forgive us our debts, as we forgive our debtors" (Matthew 6:12).

Any hatred that is harbored in our heart toward others, for any reason, arouses an anti-Christ spirit that rebels in every way against God. You must forgive your husband, your wife, your children, and anyone who has wounded you. You must forgive all of them completely before the sweet spirit of Christ can possess your heart and control your life.

Many times forgiveness seems impossible due to the grievous offense that occurred and as human beings we aren't able to naturally forgive. However, when we ask God to give us the spirit of forgiveness we are then able, in His precious name, to give and receive its healing balm. The bitter feeling in our heart is removed, and God will replace it with His perfect peace. But first we must ask!

ACCEPTING JESUS AS SAVIOR IS A MUST!

There is no deliverance without surrender. The tormented soul must surrender their life to Christ or there is no point in continuing. In fact, no person is truly free or protected from the wiles of the Devil without confessing Jesus as Lord and Savior. Below is a sample prayer:

Satan, I denounce you, your Kingdom, and your demon spirits. I reject your rule and refuse to be dominated by your tormenting evil spirits any longer. I accept Jesus Christ as my Lord and Savior. You no longer have dominion over me. I am now a child of God! Amen.

LIFE AFTER DELIVERANCE

Finally and most importantly, every delivered person must unequivocally break any and all relationships that connected them to demonic powers. They should become involved in a Bible study or a prayer group, and seek out Christian fellowship. Demons have the ability to return, and if the delivered person's heart is not filled with the presence and authority of Jesus Christ, then demonic powers will reign once again (Matthew 12:43–45).

Remember: we are at war! Every Christian is engaged in spiritual combat. When believers put on the whole armor of God (Ephesians 6:11), all the demons in hell can't conquer us. We have been given absolute authority over Satan and his demonic monsters. The Bible declares, "Resist the devil and he will flee from you" (James 4:7)! Acknowledge that Satan is alive, learn to recognize his evil influence, and then take action to defeat him with the power of the Holy Spirit and the authority of Jesus' name.

Never forget this truth: "He who is in you is greater than he who is in the world" (1 John 4:4). And believe with all your heart and mind that the Lord has created a multitude of angels whose commission it is to guard, protect, defend, and minister to God's children.

We are surrounded by a heavenly host of angels—God's very elect!

12
The Elect Angels

I charge you before God and the Lord Jesus Christ
and the elect angels . . .
—1 TIMOTHY 5:21

The supernatural deliverance that angels provide is part of the salvation God has given to those who have accepted His Son as Savior. Salvation means deliverance, preservation, healing, and soundness. Angels are the agents of God Almighty who deliver and protect us from peril, who bring God's healing balm to our spirit and comfort to our souls. The believer has the ability to summon the aid of angels as part of our salvation.[1]

In order to understand what role angels play in this world—and more specifically, in your personal life—we must first understand who angels are.

ANGELS ARE SUPERNATURAL BEINGS

For by Him all things were created that are in heaven and that are on earth, visible and invisible [including angels], whether thrones or dominions or principalities or powers. All things were created through Him and for Him. (Colossians 1:16)

Angels are usually invisible to us; therefore, we often don't acknowledge their presence. However, Paul states the things that are not seen are greater than the things that are seen (2

Corinthians 4:18), which means the invisible world of the supernatural is far greater than this temporal world in which we live.

Angels exist and minister in the Third Heaven *and* on earth. They serve God and man alike. The sheer thought of this fact should cause you to tremble. One moment they are in the physical presence of God—the Creator of all—and the next they are ministering to us here on earth.

ANGELS ARE WITHOUT NUMBER

But you have come to Mount Zion and to the city of the living God, the heavenly Jerusalem, to an innumerable company of angels. (Hebrews 12:22)

The book of Hebrews speaks of an "innumerable company of angels" (12:22). Why did God create so many angels? Because, His Word declares that, "He shall give His *angels* [plural] charge over you, to keep you in all your ways" (Psalm 91:11). God will use as many angels as needed to protect and care for His children.

Remember, the things that are unseen are greater than the things that are seen. Psalm 34:7 tells us, "The angel of the LORD encamps all around those who fear Him, and delivers them." The word *encamp* means "to constantly encircle." That means the angels of God are positioned where you are, and they stand wingtip to wingtip with their swords drawn. They are prepared to defend the righteous because we are the property of God. The angels have the power and authority to defend us with the supernatural power that God affords them!

ANGELS—THE CHARIOTS OF FIRE

Suddenly a chariot of fire appeared with horses of fire, and separated the two of them; and Elijah went up by a whirlwind into heaven. (2 Kings 2:11)

I've read dozens of theology books, and they all say angels fly fast. Well, just how fast is fast? Jesus is called the "Angel of the Lord" in the Old Testament. Look at what Jesus said to Mary, who came to the tomb following His resurrection and apparently tried to embrace the risen Christ when she recognized Him. Jesus told her, "Do not cling to Me, for I have not yet ascended to My Father; but go to My brethren and say to them, 'I am ascending to My Father and your Father, and to My God and your God'" (John 20:17).

Jesus went to Heaven and came back later that day, because two verses later, He appears in the Upper Room and hails the disciples as friends (v. 19). So that means Jesus went to Heaven and back in about a half a day.

We know that the Third Heaven is beyond the North Star, so let's use the North Star as a measuring rod. The North Star is 323 light-years away from earth. A light-year is the distance that light travels in one year, which is 186,000 miles per second. The light you see coming from the North Star tonight has been on its way for 323 years, going 186,000 miles a second. Now you double the number 323, because that's just one way. Jesus went there and back, so He went at least 646 light years faster than 186,000 miles per second! Jesus is saying that angels can travel at supersonic speed in a single day! That is simply beyond comprehension.

ANGELS HAVE AWESOME POWER

And of the angels He says: "Who makes His angels spirits and His ministers a flame of fire." (Hebrews 1:7)

Angels are mighty in power, and they execute the judgment of God. We can observe their astounding power in Revelation 9:15: "So the four angels, who had been prepared for the hour and day and month and year, were released to kill a third of mankind." Now think about that. At some point in the future during the Great Tribulation, God is going to use the angels to destroy one-third of the human race in twenty-four hours. The year, the month, the day, and the hour for that judgment has already been selected.

A second demonstration of the angels' power is found in Revelation 14:19–20: "So the angel thrust his sickle [a sickle in biblical times was a razor-sharp scythe that was held with two hands and used to cut grain in the wheat field] into the earth and gathered the vine of the earth, and threw *it* into the great winepress of the wrath of God. And the winepress was trampled outside the city [Jerusalem], and blood came out of the winepress, up to the horses' bridles, for one thousand six hundred furlongs [200 miles]." The apostle Paul tells us that at that point, "all Israel will be saved" (Romans 11:26). The Bible says that God has given the mighty archangel Michael the command to defend Israel and the Jewish people (Daniel 12:1).

ANGELS HEED GOD'S WORD

Bless the LORD, you His angels, who excel in strength, who do His word, heeding the voice of His word. (Psalm 103:20)

God designed angels to listen to the voice of His Word. They are governed by His precepts, and it is the angels' duty to do what God assigns them to do.

For God's Word to be fulfilled on earth, we, as His vessels, must speak His Word in faith in order for the angels to be put into action. When we speak in agreement with God's Word, the angels will go before us and prosper us in every area of our life. However, if we speak contrary to God's Word, we nullify the ability of the angels to minister to us. Unbelief binds. Speaking doubt, fear, worry, anxiety is opposing God's Word and an affront to the angels assigned to us. Our lack of faith binds and provokes angels instead of releasing them to help accomplish God's glorious will in our life.[2]

It was Elisha who released the angels to protect and defend Israel by declaring, "Do not fear, for those who are with us are more than those who are with them" (2 Kings 6:16). God provided supernatural deliverance because of the words Elisha spoke. He could have provoked the angels by using words of doubt and unbelief, but instead the angels came to his defense because Elisha had faith in God to move a legion of angels on his behalf and on the behalf of the nation of Israel.

ANGELS ARE ASSIGNED TO DELIVER

The angel of the LORD encamps all around those who fear Him, and delivers them. (Psalm 34:7)

When you are God's child, the angels of heaven will make your enemy their enemy and your adversary their adversary. God will turn His angels loose on your enemies.

Let me illustrate this. A number of years ago a man in my

church—a godly man who raised his children in the church—came to me concerning his son, who was selling illegal drugs. The father said, "My son has given his heart to Christ and has told these drug dealers that he wants to quit working for them, but they have said they will kill him if he does. What shall I do?"

I said, "Let's use the Esther model. Invite these men to your house for supper." His eyes opened wide, as I continued, "During dinner, tell them that your son has given his heart to Christ. Inform them that you are his spiritual authority and that your home and family are under the protection of God Almighty and His powerful angels. And then tell them that for their own well-being they should leave your son alone."

The father looked at me with unbelief and said, "Pastor, I don't think they will receive that."

I told him, "It doesn't matter whether they receive the truth or not. You are the spiritual authority over your household and as the head of your family when you make a divine proclamation, the angels of God record it in heaven. If these men continue to pursue your son they are guilty of offending heaven. At the very moment you declare His protection over your son, God is bound by His Word to release the angels of heaven to defend him from the evil that surrounds him. Once God and His angels are involved, things are going to turn around."

So he did exactly what I suggested. He and his wife prepared a delicious meal and invited the hoodlums to dinner. At the end of the evening the father delivered the divine proclamation, and the criminals laughed in his face, mocked his comments, and slammed the door as they angrily left his home. God will not be ridiculed, for the Word says, "Do not be deceived, God is not mocked; for whatever a man sows, that he will also reap" (Galatians 6:7). Within ninety days, all three men who had tormented his son were dead, killed in three single-vehicle collisions.

God has made a promise to the righteous: He will give His angels charge over you to keep you in all your ways.

ANGELS ARE WATCHING

For we have been made a spectacle to the world, both to angels and to men. (1 Corinthians 4:9)

Spectacle originates from the Latin word *spectaculum*, which means "public show." It was during the first-century that athletes were put on display, and fans—similar to modern-day sports fanatics—cheered passionately for their favorite athlete.

I ask you, who is watching over our lives? Hebrews 12:1 tells us, "We are surrounded by so great a cloud of witnesses." This "great cloud" refers to the angels of God who observe our every move. They are intensely watching our lives because our God is so very passionate about His children. He's our biggest fan and the angels follow suit!

The Bible proclaims that God "shall give his *angels* [plural] charge over you" (Psalm 91:11). Therefore, every believer, based on Scripture, has been assigned at least two or more angels to watch, to guard, and to defend us. Furthermore, angels also witness how we interact with fellow believers. Paul writes in 1 Timothy 5:21, "I charge you before God and the Lord Jesus Christ and the elect angels that you observe these things, . . . doing nothing with partiality." Everything that is done to us or by us is being recorded in the heavenlies by our Father, His Son, and the host of angels assigned to watch over us.

ANGELS PROTECT

For He shall give His angels charge over you, to keep you in all your ways. In their hands they shall bear you up, lest you dash your foot against a stone. (Psalm 91:11–12)

This Scripture verse has been a source of great comfort throughout the many years I have served the Lord.

When I left home to attend Bible college in Waxahachie, Texas, my parents prayed a prayer of blessing, gave me seventy-five dollars, and informed me that all future financial responsibilities were mine. Subsequently, I paid for my tuition and living expenses by being a guest preacher in churches throughout Texas, Oklahoma, and Arkansas. Most Friday afternoons after classes ended, I would pack a small overnight bag, place it in the backseat of my used 1955 Plymouth Belvedere four-door sedan, and drive to the rally or camp meeting where I was invited to preach—and I was grateful for every opportunity.

The rallies would often last long into the night. I either stayed in the home of the hosting pastor or, when I could afford it, I overnighted at a nearby motel. Depending on the distance from the university, I would leave the rally with just enough time to pull into my dormitory parking lot, take a quick shower, and run to class on Monday morning. I was especially exhausted after one particular weekend when I had preached nearly nonstop for three straight days. There wasn't an opportunity to stay over that night, and so I immediately left following the services to begin my long drive home.

The road back to Waxahachie from Oklahoma was flat and tedious, and the hum of the tires rolling down the highway caused me to drift off to sleep behind the steering wheel.

Suddenly, I was shaken out of my slumber with the booming sound of the car hitting some railroad tracks! I tightly held on to the wheel as a drowning man would a life preserver while my car sailed in midair! Then, as if in slow motion, I landed miraculously in my own lane just as an eighteen-wheel gas tanker whizzed past me coming from the opposite direction. I was now wide awake as a jolt of adrenaline rushed through my body!

I was stunned at what had occurred. How was it possible to lose control of a car, become airborne, and then land several feet down the road as if nothing had happened? Only God's angels could have provided me with this supernatural protection that spared me from the otherwise devastating outcome. I spent the rest of the drive praising God and keeping both eyes wide open!

Early the next morning, I heard banging on my dorm room door as I prepared for class. My roommate informed me that my mother was on the phone. I rarely received social calls from home, so I ran to the phone, hoping all was well. After a short greeting, Vada Hagee began to interrogate me as only she could: "Where were you last night?"

I told her about the church rally and then the story of the soaring Belvedere. She was silent for a few seconds and asked if I was all right. Then she questioned me further about the exact time of the incident. "Just after one o'clock in the morning," I responded.

My mother then recounted the following story: "I was awakened abruptly with a deep sense of urgency to intercede for you. I knew you must have been in some sort of trouble and I began earnestly seeking the Lord and proclaiming Psalm 91 on your behalf asking God to send His angels to protect you. Once I felt

His peace I went back to bed and slept like a baby. That was just a little before 1:00 a.m. John, I believe the Lord woke me so I could pray for your safety and He in turn charged His angels to come to your aid."

ANGELS WORSHIP

And they do not rest day or night, saying: "Holy, holy, holy, Lord God Almighty, Who was and is and is to come!" (Revelation 4:8)

The primary purposes of angels are to worship the Lord, to be the attendants to the throne of God, and to be the guardians to the church (believers). Angels do not need a Savior, but they do rejoice in the redemption and salvation of sinners, and they declare the infinite merits of the Lord Jesus as the Lamb of God for sinners slain. Angels announce in the heavens that Jesus is worthy to receive "power and riches and wisdom, and strength and honor and glory and blessing" (Revelation 5:12).

Then I looked, and I heard the voice of many angels around the throne, the living creatures, and the elders; and the number of them was ten thousand times ten thousand, and thousands of thousands saying with a loud voice:
"Worthy is the Lamb who was slain
To receive power and riches and wisdom,
And strength and honor and glory and blessing!"
—Revelation 5:11–12

Our Inheritance

For I am the LORD your God. You shall therefore consecrate
yourselves, and you shall be holy; for I am holy.
—LEVITICUS 11:44

God desires that His church attain our divine inheritance as
"heirs of God and joint heirs with Christ" (Romans 8:17). In
earthly inheritances only the firstborn are heirs, but the church
is a church of firstborn—we are *all heirs*. Every believer will
inherit heaven. We do not gain our entry into this divine inheritance by what we do or who we know or how much we can
afford. It is purely by a loving act of God that we are made heirs
to our eternal home.

Christ, as Mediator, is said to be the heir of all things
(Hebrews 1:2). He is the portion of the saints' inheritance
(Psalm 16:5), and true believers, by virtue of their union with
Him, shall inherit all things (Revelation 21:7).[1]

My prayer is that the knowledge you have gained through
this study, which has confirmed the existence of all Three
Heavens and the workings of the supernatural, will help you
take the necessary steps to ensure that you and your household
are saved and sanctified—for the day of the Lord draws near.

Notes

Chapter 1: *Week 1:* What Are the Three Heavens?

1. Dr. Jack Cleary, quoted in North Central Baptist Hospital video, *Mission Moment: The Jackson Kreye Story* (2008), https://docs.google.com /file/d/0ByeoS4kB6d21UjBPV2hYXzV3d0E/edit?pli=1.

2. *Oxford Dictionary*, s.v. "miracle," http://www.oxforddictionaries.com/us/definition /american_english/miracle.

3. William Smith, *Smith's Bible Dictionary*, s.v. "miracles," accessed October 3, 2015, http://www.ntslibrary.com/PDF%20Books/Smith's%20Bible%20Dictionary.pdf.

4. Matthew George Easton, *Illustrated Bible Dictionary*, 3rd ed. (Nashville: Thomas Nelson, 1897), s.v. "heaven," http://www.studylight.org/dictionaries/ebd/view.cgi?n=1704.

Chapter 2: *Week 2:* Creation: The First Heaven

1. John Phillips, *Exploring Genesis: An Expository Commentary* (Grand Rapids: Kregel, 2001), 38.

2. *Four Blood Moons*, directed by Kieth Merrill, performed by Dennis Prager (a Goose Creek Production presented by FBM Productions, LLC, in association with Reelworks Studio, LLC and the WTA Group, 2015), DVD.

3. John Hagee, *Invasion of Demons: The Battle Between God and Satan in Our Time* (Old Tappan, NJ: Fleming H. Revell, 1973), 93.

4. John Hagee, *From Daniel to Doomsday* (Nashville: Thomas Nelson, 1999), 221.

5. John Hagee, *Four Blood Moons: Something Is About to Change* (Brentwood, TN: Worthy, 2013), 17–18.

6. Matthew George Easton, *Illustrated Bible Dictionary*, 3rd ed. (Nashville: Thomas Nelson, 1897), s.v. "Daystar," accessed October 3, 2015, https://www.biblegateway.com /resources/eastons-bible-dictionary/daystar.

7. John Hagee, "I See Heaven," *The Three Heavens* (San Antonio, TX: John Hagee Ministries, 2015), DVD.

8. Hagee, *Four Blood Moons*, 34.

9. "Earth's Moon: Our Natural Satellite," National Aeronautics and Space Administration Solar System Exploration, accessed October 3, 2015, http://solarsystem.nasa.gov /planets/profile.cfm?Object=Moon&Display=OverviewLong.

10. Hagee, *Four Blood Moons*, 43–44.

Chapter 3: *Week 3:* Spiritual War in the Second Heaven

1. *Vine's Greek New Testament Dictionary*, s.v. "mesouranema," accessed October 3, 2015, http://gospelhall.org/bible/bible.php?search=mesouranema&dict=vine&lang=greek#A1.

2. "The Fall of Day Star," Let Us Reason Ministries, accessed October 3, 2015, http://www.letusreason.org/Biblexp227.htm.

3. James Orr, gen. ed., *International Standard Bible Encyclopedia* (1915), s.v. "cherubim," accessed October 3, 2015, http://www.biblestudytools.com/dictionary/cherubim-1/.

4. Walter A. Elwell, ed., *Baker's Evangelical Dictionary of Biblical Theology* (Grand Rapids: Baker, 1996), s.v. "Satan," by Walter M. Dunnett, accessed October 3, 2015, http://www.biblestudytools.com/dictionary/satan/.

5. Charles H. Spurgeon, "Evening —June 3," in *Morning and Evening: Daily Readings*, vol. 1 (Charleston, SC: BiblioBazaar, 2008), 362–63.

Chapter 4: *Week 4:* Invasion of Demons in Society and the Church

1. Entertainment Software Rating Board, "ESRB Ratings Guide," accessed October 3, 2015, http://www.esrb.org/ratings/ratings_guide.jsp.

2. Catherine Beyer, "Tarot Cards and How Tarot Readings Work," About Religion, accessed October 3, 2015, http://altreligion.about.com/od/ritualsandpractices/a/tarot.htm.

Chapter 5: *Week 5:* Evil and the Antichrist

1. Benjamin Radford, "The Science (and the Non-Science) of the Ouija Board," Discovery News, October 24, 2014, http://news.discovery.com/human/the-science-and-non-science-of-the-ouija-141024.htm.

2. "2 Corinthians 10:3–5 Commentary," Precept Austin, last updated February 21, 2015, http://www.preceptaustin.org/2corinthians_103-5_exposition.htm.

3. John Hagee, *Four Blood Moons: Something Is About to Change* (Brentwood, TN: Worthy, 2013), 194–95.

Chapter 6: *Week 6:* Deliver Us from the Evil One

1. Charles Ryrie, *So Great Salvation* (Wheaton, IL: Victor, 1989), 59–60.

Chapter 7: *Week 7:* Where Angels Tread

1. Douglas D. Webster, *Follow the Lamb: A Pastoral Approach to the Revelation* (Eugene, OR: Wipf and Stock, 2014), 156.

Chapter 8: *Week 8: The Third Heaven*

1. John Hagee, *The Revelation of Truth: A Mosaic of God's Plan for Man* (Nashville: Thomas Nelson, 2000), 276–77.

2. Ibid., 279–80.

Chapter 10: Identifying Demons

1. Mary C. Norton, *Demon Experiences in Many Lands: A Compilation,* comp. Kenneth Nathanial Taylor (Chicago: Moody, 1960), 56.

2. Verne Roberts, *Demon Experiences,* comp. Taylor, 67–69.

3. Adapted from Frances D. Manuel, *Though an Host Should Encamp* (Fort Washington, PA: Christian Literature Crusade, 1971), 174–76.

4. James E. Russell, *Demon Experience,* comp. Taylor, 50.

Chapter 12: The Elect Angels

1. Charles and Annette Capps, *Angels* (England, AR: Capps Publishing, 1984), 133.

2. Portions adapted from Charles and Annette Capps, *Angels,* 83, 88, 113–14, 116–17.

Our Inheritance

1. Matthew Henry, *Matthew Henry's Concise Commentary on the Whole Bible* (Nashville: Thomas Nelson, 1997), 1066–95.

Sources Referenced

- Hagee, John. *The Three Heavens* DVD. San Antonio, TX: John Hagee Ministries, 2015.
- Hagee, John. *Four Blood Moons: Something Is About to Change.* Brentwood, TN: Worthy, 2013.
- Hagee, John. *From Daniel to Doomsday.* Nashville: Thomas Nelson, 1999.
- Hagee, John. *Invasion of Demons: The Battle Between God and Satan in Our Time.* Old Tappan, NJ: Fleming H. Revell, 1973.
- Hagee, John. *The Revelation of Truth: A Mosaic of God's Plan for Man.* Nashville: Thomas Nelson, 2000.
- Hagee, John. *The Three Heavens: Angels, Demons and What Lies Ahead.* Brentwood, TN: Worthy, 2015.

DISCOVER MORE

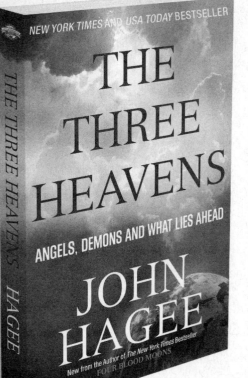
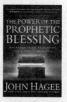